LET'S START A CIRCUS

Anders Enevig

 VAN NOSTRAND REINHOLD COMPANY

New York   Cincinnati   Toronto   London   Melbourne

A

Van Nostrand Reinhold Company Regional Offices:
New York   Cincinnati   Chicago   Millbrae   Dallas

Van Nostrand Reinhold Company International Offices:
London   Toronto   Melbourne

This book was originally published in Danish
under the title *Vi Leger Cirkus*
by Høst & Søns Forlag,
Copenhagen, Denmark

Copyright © *Vi Leger Cirkus*
Høst & Søns Forlag 1971
English translation © Van Nostrand
Reinhold Company Ltd. 1973

Library of Congress Catalog Card
Number 72 9722
ISBN 0 442 29975 3

Translated from the Danish by Joan Bulman
Cover photograph by Anders Enevig
Line drawings by Grete Petersen
This book is printed in Great Britain
by Jolly & Barber Ltd., Rugby
and bound by the Ferndale Book Company

Published by Van Nostrand Reinhold Company Inc.
450 West 33rd St., New York, N.Y. 10001
and Van Nostrand Reinhold Company Ltd.
25–28 Buckingham Gate, London SW1E 6LQ

Published simultaneously in Canada by
Van Nostrand Reinhold Company Ltd.

16   15   14   13   12   11   10   9   8   7   6   5   4   3   2   1

CONTENTS

Preface for Grown-up Children

Children's games often reflect cultural history for good or ill. One doesn't need to look very far to find concrete examples in such fields as war and exploration. Cowboys and Indians reflects the white man's conquest of North America, and the battle between society and law-breakers is re-enacted in the game of Cops and Robbers.

But children's games also involve everyday happenings that are never mentioned in history books but have left their mark and given children material for their games.

Children of all ages have always dreamt of the world of travelling jugglers and circus people, and have the advantage of being able to copy the arts of particular kinds of people in their games.

The makers of children's toys have seldom bothered with

Young artists. Illustration from Les Jeux du Cirque et la Vie Foraine *(Paris, 1889).*

5

these everyday games, but have left children the challenge of using their imagination to make the equipment they need for themselves.

This book is *not* an elementary introduction to the art of the circus, but I hope it may help to whet your appetite for the living circus. The material has been gathered over a period of ten years, partly by watching children playing circus on the lawn or in the playground, and partly by visiting large and small circuses and juggling performances. But even so it would never have come into being without the help of other people who shared my interest, and I would like to thank everyone who contributed, including the two acrobats on the cover, Lone and Charlotte Høstrup of Odense.

I am particularly indebted to the following experts for good ideas and practical help: Martin, Eva and Erling Larsen of Allesø on Funen, who toured during the summer with the Star Circus, and other travelling shows, under the professional name of Waldini; Erico Lund of Copenhagen, better known as the Pierrot at Dyrehavsbakken, who, outside the summer season, works as a freelance Pierrot, in Punch and Judy shows, as a Father Christmas, and is a ventriloquist, clown and singer of some renown; Hans Høstrup of Odense, who has several times been the ring-master of a children's circus and whose professional name is Ricy the Illusionist; Peter Grønbæck of Copenhagen, who rides round Denmark on a three-wheeled transport cycle as the Juggler Cibrino and shows performing parrots and rats; and last but not least, my wife, Inga Enevig, who appeared as an eleven-year-old in a children's circus in Store Heddinge as a ballet dancer and veil dancer. Since then she has been a keen circus-goer, and has been a great help to me in preparing this book.

ANDERS ENEVIG

We start a Children's Circus

Our circus is a game, but we want to make it as close to a real circus as possible.

Once we have made up our minds to get up a circus, there will be lots of things to do. Here is a list of some of them:

Choosing the ring-master
Deciding the roles
Equipment and training
What is the circus to be called?
Posters, programmes and tickets

Costumes
Make-up
Music
Ring, curtain and changing room
Dress rehearsal
First night

Some years ago 300 old sacks were converted into a two-pole tent by some children at Hjør-ring. A good used sack was accepted as payment for a ticket. The ring was enclosed by planks set on edge and supported by pegs hammered into the ground.

A list of circus acts will be found on p. 39. And now, let's get started!

This ring-master is from the Circus Zoo, Odense.

Choosing the ring-master

It is best to have a rather older boy or girl as ring-master, someone who everyone agrees will be good at getting things going. But it is also important that he or she should be practical and full of ideas, because there are so many things to attend to before the performance can take place.

So it is very important to choose the right person, and preferably someone who is keen on circuses and has seen a real performance.

If the ring-master is a girl, she can wear a striking dress in the ring. Either a long evening dress or a blouse and mini-skirt would be suitable, or she could wear a white blouse with long long black trousers and a top hat, which looks very effective.

If we are to keep to the circus tradition, a boy's choice is more limited as regards clothes. He can wear, for example, a pair of long dark trousers and a white shirt with a bow tie. Possibly also a home-made black top hat and a black moustache. This can be either a neat little toothbrush one or a big, black, handlebar moustache from the 1890s.

The ring-master always carries a tin whistle in his pocket, as this can be very useful at the right time and place.

His whip is constructed according to the principle that the larger the ring, the longer the whip and cord, the louder the crack.

A good whip for our purposes can be made from a piece of stick about 20 in. long, with a groove cut round at one end. Tie a piece of string round this, about $4\frac{1}{2}$ ft. Unravel about 6 in. at the end, and tie a knot where the unravelling begins.

Here is a little tip that will save time and cord: before cutting off the cord, 'loop up' about 10 in. at the top, as shown in the drawings, and only after that cut off the cord to the desired length, about $4\frac{1}{2}$ ft.

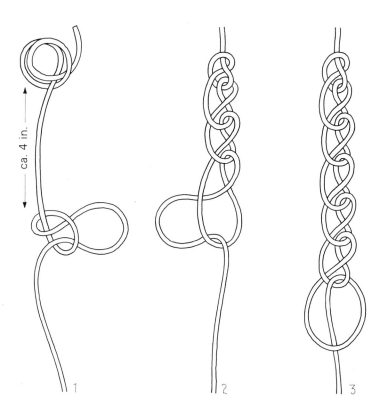

ca. 4 in.

1   2   3

This is how to 'loop-up' the whip.

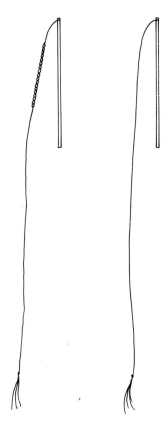

A piece of thick string will give a very soft sound, something harder, like picture cord, will give a sharper crack. A still louder and sharper crack will be obtained from a piece of $\frac{1}{8}$ in. plastic covered nylon clothes line. Remove the plastic from about the last 6 in., leaving the white nylon thread exposed, and in this case a knot will not be necessary.

As in a real circus, the ring-master must practise so as to get complete control over his whip and must only crack it verti-cally. He must not hit the horses or the audience, as it can be very dangerous to be hit in the eye by a whip lash.

If he really works hard with the whip, the cord will fray away at the end and soon become too short and have to be thrown away.

Gradually as the end wears away, undo the 'looped-up' part at the top, so that the cord always remains a steady 3–5 ft. long. The 'looping-up' represents a reserve of at least 3 ft. of cord – which is enough for a good many cracks!

Ring-master's whip. On the right in its simplest form. On the left with 'looping-up', which can be undone as the tip wears away.

Distributing the roles

Once the ring-master has been chosen, the group must decide on the distribution of the other roles.

It is important to draw as many people as possible into the game. Down to and including the little three-year-old, who can toddle around as an interval clown with a red nose and a balloon.

Some of the bigger ones may be good at dancing, others will have tired of cycling tricks in the playground; one may be particularly good at balancing, and perhaps there will be someone with a flair for conjuring tricks.

Obviously everyone will choose what he or she likes doing best. But if in the end there are not enough items to fill a programme, the ring-master will have to intervene even at this early stage and ask some of the group to make themselves responsible for some particular acts or duties.

You will also need circus hands and some of those taking part will have to undertake making posters and other practical jobs behind the scenes.

Equipment and training

Once the roles have been handed out each individual will know what he needs. And so begins the hunt to obtain equipment, the performers' tools.

Perhaps you will have to get hold of a set of rings, a trapeze and somewhere to hang them up during training.

Others may need an oil drum for balancing on, balloons, conjuring sets, ropes for tightropes, weights, a monocycle (a one-wheeled cycle) and so on.

You will certainly also have to make your own horses and obtain materials for a ring and changing room, and to find out where you can borrow benches, stools, chairs or packing cases for seats as well as a tarpaulin and a pair of curtains.

All this should be seen to in good time, so that you don't suddenly find that something is missing at the last minute.

In the meantime, you must start your training. And here the thing is to be persistent and go on trying again and again when something goes wrong. Because it will.

It may well happen that somebody will regret having chosen his particular act. It may perhaps turn out to be more difficult than he thought it was going to be.

But here it will be the duty of the ring-master to keep up his enthusiasm and encourage him to go on.

It is important even at this stage for the performers and the ring-master himself to practise how to make their entrance into the ring, how to greet the audience and how, after presenting their act, to bow or curtsy to the audience and leave the ring.

What to call the circus?

One of the first problems we shall come up against is what are we going to call the circus? There are a great many possibilities, but the choice is really quite limited, because the name must both sound good and be easy to read on the posters.

Many circuses have been called after their manager, either by his real name or his professional name: Altenburg, Price, Bertram Mills, Billy Smart, Hofmann, Althoff, Miller, Rolando, Belli and Sarrasani. These are names that go very well with the word 'circus'.

When a circus is named after its manager, it is because he is the owner of the business, but as there is no 'owner' of our circus, there is no reason to use the manager's name. It is best to choose a neutral but impressive name. Here are a few suggestions to give you some ideas. They are names of former and existing circuses: the Crown Circus, the Arena Circus, the Olympia Circus, Star, Lion, Astoria, Royal, Zoo, Safari and Apollo.

Posters, programmes and tickets

Publicity is very important to a circus, so a great deal should be made of posters, programmes and handbills.

The purpose of a *poster* is to let people know that there is a circus in town.

For a poster to be effective, several things are necessary: it must not be too small, not less than 15 in. × 25 in., it must be painted in strong colours, so that it hits the eye, and the word 'CIRCUS' must be clearly visible from a distance.

There are several kinds of circus poster.

Some have a large circus motif as an eye-catcher, such as a rearing horse or a clown's face. Others have smaller motifs in bright colours with a list of the names of the artistes and the acts.

It is important to think up strange and impressive-sounding names for the poster. The performers taking part might, for

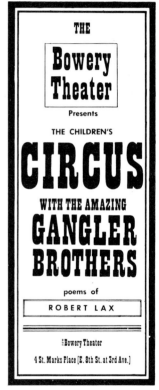

Poster for the Children's Circus held in the Bowery Theater in New York in 1961–2. The Circus was originally planned to run for two weeks over Christmas, but was so successful that it continued at the weekends until March.

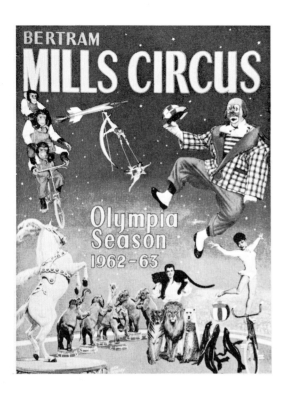

This poster for Bertram Mills's 1962–3 season in London shows how you can produce eye-catching publicity by including lots of different acts on your poster.

Right: an amusing poster designed by Erik Stockmarr of Copenhagen.

instance, be called The Mazurka Sisters, Les Palmedos, Mr Gordon, Two Santos, Mr Everest, Miss China, Tonelli, Marian Gitano, Antonio Bros, Bob Stone, Leontini, Four Sioux, etc.

The poster must always give clear information as to:
1. The name of the circus.
2. The time and place of the performance.
3. The price of tickets for children and grown-ups.

You can use potato prints or linocuts for both posters and programmes. Possibly someone has facilities for getting playbills duplicated, so that they can be distributed in the neighbourhood or at school.

Tickets can be simply small numbered pieces of paper. Remember that there must be one kind for children and another for grown-ups. A tear-off block of printed numbers can be bought quite cheaply from a stationer's, and these blocks are obtainable in different colours.

Programmes can be done on a typewriter with carbon copies, or duplicated. If you can get hold of a spirit duplicator, it is nice to include drawings on the programme.

Here are some suggestions for a programme. The great thing is to make the numbers as varied and exciting as possible.

1. Marksman Buffalo Bill and the Indian girl Bright Star.
2. The world-famous clowns Larno and Splint.
3. Strong man and weight-lifter Mr Minalka.
4. Veil dancers Karina, Jeanette, Rositta and Isabella.
5. Star dancer Mr Tango and Miss Sylvia.
6. The Silvana Sisters, trapeze artists.

Poster for Don Ross's Circus. Of course you won't be using real lions, but it's a good idea to show the ring-master on your posters.

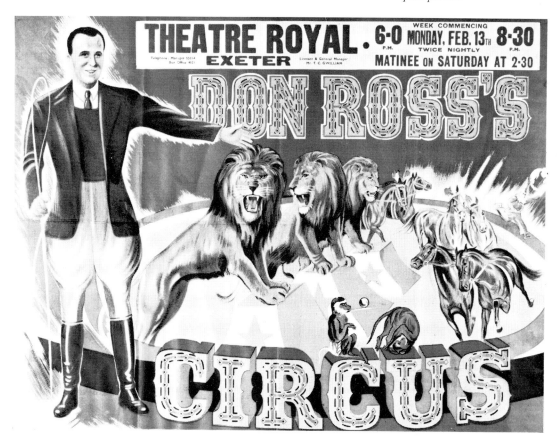

THEATRE ROYAL. 6·0 WEEK COMMENCING 8·30
P.M. MONDAY, FEB. 13TH P.M.
EXETER TWICE NIGHTLY
MATINEE ON SATURDAY AT 2·30

DON ROSS'S

CIRCUS

7. Mr Jackson, lasso artist.
8. Romany dancers Marietta and Esmeralda.
9. Juggler Mr Wåhlberg from Norrköping.
10. Indian Chief Deerfoot with his warriors.
11. Miss Elvira, the intrepid tightrope walker.
12. Snake girl and contortionist, Miss Miranda.
13. Merlin, the famous magician and wizard.

If one of the performers or stage-hands is good at writing poems, make your programme extra special by including a circus poem. This is part of the programme sold by the Children's Circus at the Bowery Theater in New York.

As with real circus programmes, it should conclude with the sentence: 'The management reserves the right to make alterations in the programme'.

You can do as much or as little publicity as you like, but the more advertising you do, the more people will come.

If it starts pouring with rain just as the programme is due to start, put up a notice board at the entrance stating the day and time at which the postponed performance will take place. This is the best solution, for it is no fun for the performers or the audience to carry on in pouring rain.

Costumes

The costumes should not cost a lot of money. In general, you ought to be able to manage with what you can rummage out of drawers and cupboards, using old and discarded clothes.

Some of the things will certainly be too big, but they can be adapted with the help of safety pins and a few stitches. Here it will certainly be an advantage to have a grown-up to help.

You can do great things to brighten up an otherwise rather tired-looking dress with the help of crêpe paper, which can be bought from a stationer's in a wide range of colours.

14

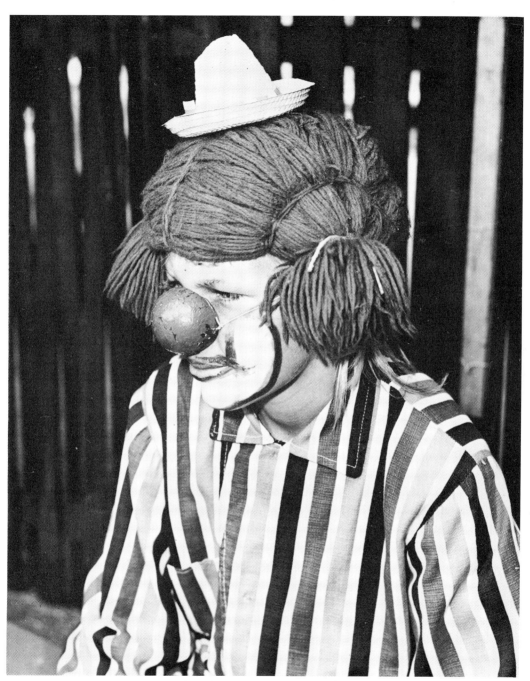

Clown from the Circus Zoo, Odense. A smart pair of striped pyjamas, a wool wig, a red cardboard nose – and behold your clown!

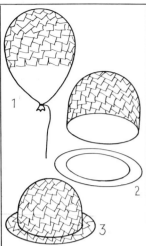

A bowler hat can be made of papier mâché or, better still, of 'gauze mâché' (see p. 26). It is made over a blown-up balloon. Take care not to make it too big. Measure the circumference as for other hats. Glue a few layers of pieces of gauze – the size of match boxes – over the balloon (fig. 1). The gauze will dry out overnight, and the balloon will collapse by itself. Cut out a cardboard brim as for the other hats (fig. 2). Then attach the brim to the crown with gauze and glue (fig. 3). Paint the hat black with, for example, poster paint. Or you can varnish it with clear matt varnish. The curls of a wig can be glued inside the hat (see p. 25).

Hats

Hats can be made of cardboard to look like flat Chinese hats or perhaps pointed clowns' hats. Hats can also be bought ready-made in toyshops and in shops where they sell tricks and jokes, where incidentally you can also pick up a good many ideas simply by using your eyes. You can also buy masks there.

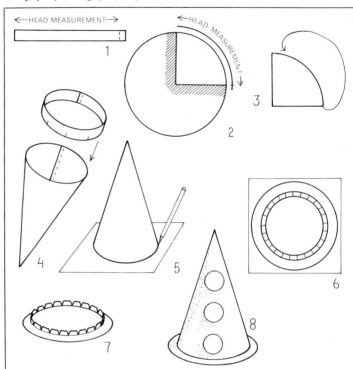

A pointed clown's hat can also be made of cardboard. Cut a strip of cardboard and measure the circumference of the head (fig. 1). Draw a large circle, a quarter of which corresponds to the head measurement. Cut this quarter out and glue it together like the Chinese hat (figs. 2 and 3). Glue the measured head band together and stick it inside the hat. If necessary, cut small nicks in this 'sweatband' so that it will slip into place more easily (fig. 4). Now stand the hat on a piece of cardboard and draw round the outside. This will be the brim (fig. 5). Now draw a larger circle outside and a smaller circle inside and cut them out (fig. 6). The inner circle is cut into notches, which are glued to the inside of the hat (figs. 7 and 8). The hat can be decorated with tinsel and white cut-out circles glued on.

A kimono, and you have the beginnings of a Chinaman. The hat is made of cardboard and the beard of black wool.

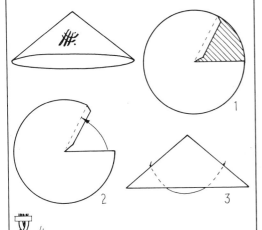

A circle cut out of cardboard makes a Chinese hat. Fig. 1 shows how a '10-minute' section is cut out. The two edges are glued one on top of the other (fig. 2), and the hat is finished (fig. 3). The dotted line shows where the elastic or tie is attached. A pigtail of plaited wool can be glued inside the hat.

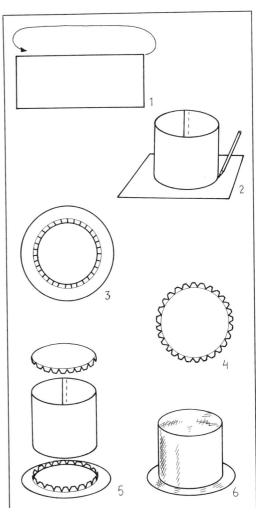

A top hat is cut out of black cardboard. Measure the head as for the pointed clown's hat and cut out a square of the height you want the hat to be and the width of the head measurement – plus a little extra, so that the edges can be glued together to make a cylinder (fig. 1). As for the clown's hat, draw round the outside of the cylinder to make a brim (figs. 2 and 3). Then draw another circle and cut darts in it, to make a top for the hat (fig. 4). Glue everything together (fig. 5).

Shoes

The clown's shoes can be made out of a couple of shoe boxes or other cardboard boxes, painted black. Glue a pair of worn-out old shoes inside the boxes, and cut a hole in the lid for the legs to go through, as shown in the illustration.

You can also lengthen a pair of old shoes that you are never going to wear again by sticking another pair of cut-off tops over the toecaps with strong glue, and then painting them red.

You can also wear a pair of straw shoes, if you can get hold of them.

A large pair of clown's shoes in violin-case size can be made out of shoe boxes. Glue an old shoe or stocking with a leather sole on to the inside of the lid (fig. 1). Cut the box as shown in fig. 2 and glue it together with a strong glue (fig. 3). Paint the shoes black or red and add a shoe lace if desired.

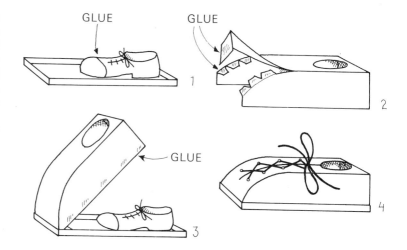

Padding

It is sometimes necessary to stuff cushions inside your clothes in order to look really big and grown-up.

Artificial bosoms can be made in various ways. You can stuff a long plastic bag full of rags etc. and tie it in the middle. Or you can use a couple of blown-up balloons which, in addition, can be punctured and will explode with a bang, as in the comic dance number with a rag doll described on p. 53.

A little girl can be made to look tall with the help of a long skirt, if she stands on a packing case of suitable size and the skirt reaches down to the ground. Of course she cannot move about too much, but she can quite well stand at the entrance to the circus and help to take the tickets.

Red Indians

A good strong feather head-dress for a Red Indian chief can be made by folding a strip of waxcloth about $4\frac{1}{2}$ ft. long by 3 in. wide down the centre lengthwise, with the wrong side out. Now sew all along the edges with linen thread, using stitches about $\frac{1}{4}$ in. long. Paint crosses and circles on the white 'wrong' side. Stitch two tapes to the back of the waxcloth so that it exactly fits round the head, and the strip hangs down the back. Stick feathers in between the stitches all along the edge at suitable intervals. Fix the feathers firmly with a few stitches and the head-dress is finished.

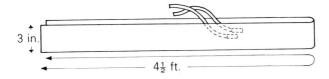

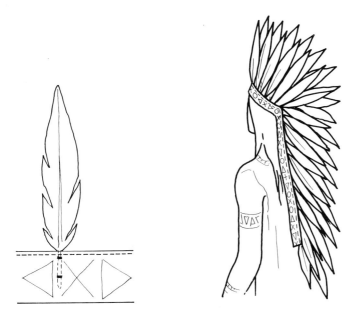

Large, strong, feather head-dress for an Indian chief.

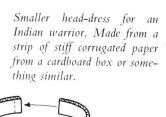

Smaller head-dress for an Indian warrior. Made from a strip of stiff corrugated paper from a cardboard box or something similar.

Head-dress for an Indian girl. Made of a band of the right width to fit a belt buckle. The feather is stuck in between the band and the centre of the buckle and placed at the back of the head.

Indian dress for a warrior made of thin sacking. The neck opening is covered with a collar and shirt front, as shown in the small drawing. The costume should be long enough for the fringe to reach to the middle of the thigh. Indian trousers can be made in the form of leggings, i.e. loose trouser-legs with fringes at the sides, and cone-shaped, as shown in the fig. to the right. They are attached to the belt by loops. For painting on sacking see p. 30.

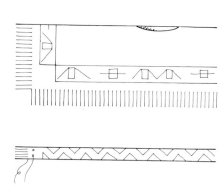

Indian dress for girls. The upper part with sleeves and the skirt are made of thin sacking. The belt can end with a fringe as shown.

Almost dyed-in-the-wool Red Indians in a lasso number with sharp-shooting as a speciality. See p. 48.

A flimsier feather head-dress can be made from a strip of corrugated paper cut crosswise. All you need to do is to stick the feathers down into the holes and glue the ends of the paper together.

For ordinary warriors or Indian women the head-dress has only one feather, at the back of the neck. For this use a head-band, which can either be a narrow strip of waxcloth or a wide tape, threaded through a belt buckle. The feather is fixed into the buckle.

Remember that Red Indians on the warpath paint their faces with black and red streaks and rings. This can be done quite easily with lipstick and mascara.

Red Indian costumes are made of thin sacking, which can be decorated with painted circles or something similar and adorned with fringes. See p. 30 for painting on sacking.

Obviously the most natural role for Red Indians is in connection with cowboys, but they can also appear in various other numbers, for instance as riders, trick cyclists or tightrope walkers.

Red Indian war-paint can look like this.

21

Dyeing feathers, sacking

If you have no pheasant's feathers or other decorative feathers to make an Indian head-dress, you can dye white feathers yourself.

Buy some ordinary spirit dye in powder form, which is obtainable in a variety of colours in small packets. It is ready for use when mixed with the proper amount of spirit. See the instructions on the packet.

You can also use ordinary water dyes or aniline dyes soluble in water, but in this case you must first remove the grease from the feathers by dipping them in spirit or acetone.

These dyes are very strong and, apart from dyeing feathers, they can be used for sacking, string, shavings, sawdust and sand.

You can also use them as a cheap paint, if you want to brighten up the cardboard fittings in the ring.

If the ring is on a cement or paved base, you can paint geometric designs or a circus motif straight on to the cement using the same sort of dye. But remember, whatever happens, to get permission first, as this sort of paint is very difficult to get off.

Staining sawdust and sand

While on this subject I should like to say a word about how to stain sawdust and sand, even though in most cases it is likely to be difficult to organize a ring with sawdust in it. It is done quite simply by putting the sawdust in a sieve and pouring the dye through. Sand is tipped straight into the dye, the surplus liquid being poured off later into another container.

Glitter

And another little tip: if you are going to use glitter for hats, costumes, accessories, lettering and so forth, always buy silver glitter. It looks effective both in daylight and artificial light and shows up from a distance. Gold glitter and glitter in other colours looks dead and black. You can buy glitter in paper packets from a stationer's, and you make it stick on by first painting the object to be decorated with glue water and then scattering the glitter on. (Glue water is made by dissolving glue powder in water. Glue powder can be bought from an artists' materials shop.)

It might be easier to buy a glitter spray. This is obtainable in tubes in various colours and is ready for use, so that you simply spray it straight from the tube on to whatever you want to decorate.

But if you want to cover a larger surface, it is cheaper to buy a bag of glitter and use glue water.

Make-up

It is very important for the performers to look colourful and attractive, so a little make-up on the face will be necessary.

It ought not to be too difficult to borrow a couple of lipsticks. If eyebrows also need touching up, you can use a cork blackened by holding it over a lighted candle, and you can also borrow eye shadow.

If someone has to have a white face, you can use ordinary baby powder or talcum as a dry make-up, patting it on with a large pad of cotton wool. It will stay on better if you smear a little cream on first.

Here is a recipe for a white grease paint which can be left on for several hours: melt a little palm butter in a small pan and stir in a little talcum powder or bismuth powder, which you can buy at a chemist's (4 oz. will be plenty).

Pour the liquid fat into a small flat tin with a lid, such as a vaseline tin. Put the lid on, and if you want it to set quickly, put the tin straight into cold water or into the refrigerator. As soon as it has set the grease-paint is ready for use.

You can make black grease-paint by stirring lampblack into the liquid white substance, or by adding it to the melted palm-butter.

Grease-paint is rubbed into the skin with the fingers, and is removed by rubbing in cleansing cream and wiping it off with a rag or a piece of kitchen roll. Cleansing cream can be bought anywhere.

You must *not* use soap to wash off grease-paint as it is not good for the skin.

Never on any account use paints such as zinc white, white lead or any other metallic colours for make-up, as they are poisonous.

It can have a serious effect on the skin if you paint yourself with watercolours or other paints in order to make yourself brown like an Arab or Indian – or black like a Negro. It would be better to use food colourings, diluted or undiluted, dabbing them on with a pad of cotton wool. By mixing them with water you can produce a variety of shades. Cocoa powder dissolved in a little water also makes good brown make-up.

Hair, bald heads and skullcaps
Wool or a tuft of cotton waste can create an admirable illusion of hair or a beard, and you can make the most delightful curls out of 'hand-planed' shavings from a carpenter's shop.

The cotton waste can be dyed with ordinary cold-water dyes, obtainable anywhere.

You could also use a handful of tow for hair and a beard, but as it is very inflammable it is better not to use this.

Artificial hair can be arranged in various ways. You can glue or stitch it inside a hat, so that the curls hang down. If the hat is made of paper or papier mâché, the hair can be attached by means of a strip of gauze or artificial resin glue (see p. 16).

If the artiste is not to wear a hat, the hair can be arranged on a skullcap, a thin cap that exactly fits the head.

A real skullcap is made of gauze or linen, so that the skin can breathe through it, but you can make one in a simpler way, as you will only be wearing it a short time.

Blow up a balloon to the size of your own head. Cut up some gauze (which you can buy by the yard in wide widths in shops that sell nursing requisites, or in narrow rolls as gauze bandages, which is rather more expensive) into pieces about the size of a match box.

Pour a little resin glue into a dish and, if necessary, add a little water. Dip the pieces of gauze into the glue or use a paint brush, and stick them on to the balloon – only to the top part, which corresponds to the top of the head. Two or three layers should be enough for this purpose. Hang the skullcap up to dry overnight, and in the morning the balloon will have gone down and thrown off the 'gauze mâché' by itself. The skullcap can then be cut to the correct size.

If it fits exactly and sits on your head firmly, there will be no need for elastic, but otherwise strengthen the skullcap at the sides with a couple of extra pieces of gauze, and when it is dry, cut holes for an elastic that will pass down round the back of the neck.

If you want to be completely or half bald, paint the skullcap with covering paint (obtainable in tubes) to look like skin, and then arrange the artificial hair or curls in place. The hair, whether it is wood shavings or cotton waste, can be stuck on to the skullcap with the white, artificial, resin glue.

It is much pleasanter to work with 'gauze mâché' than with ordinary papier mâché, and it is far more durable, even in thin layers. If you have painted the gauze, the surface will be stronger if you go over it with a clear, matt lacquer.

Noses

You can make all sorts of things out of 'gauze mâché, including masks, and you can do things to an artificial nose made out of an egg-box to make it funnier. For example, you can turn it into a turned-up snout, or make a square nose and then paint it red.

Modelling wax should *not* be used for artificial noses, as it drops off when it gets warm.

You can also make a nose out of a small red rubber ball, cutting it and fastening it on with a piece of elastic round the ears.

Beards

Beards for the ring-master, the weight-lifter and others are most easily made of cotton waste. If it is to be twisted into a moustache, stiffen it with egg white.

Beards are stuck on with spirit-gum, which you will generally be able to get at a chemist's. They can be removed with spirit.

In shops that sell make-up and theatrical accessories, you can buy crêpe hair for making beards.

Music

If you happen to have a tape recorder, it is a good idea to listen to the radio and record any striking and suitable melodies.

In the old days a brass band was considered the only proper thing for a circus, but nowadays almost any kind of music will do. But it must be lively music, to lend an air of gaiety and festivity to the occasion.

Perhaps some of the performers will have become so expert that they can perform their acts in time to music, and in that case it is important to find just the right piece.

A whole circus orchestra can be formed round just one 'proper' instrument. The two 'rhythm beaters' here are using a washing board and a drum. The orchestra may also – as here – do an act on their own as musical clowns.

27

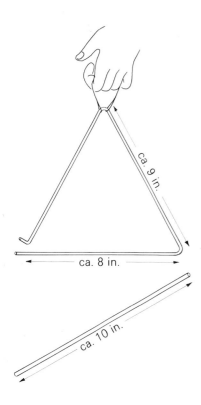

You will find it a help to record all the musical items on the tape recorder in the order in which they will be required in the performance. A record player can also be used.

The best thing of all is, of course, to have live music, if this is possible. The 'orchestra' can then be placed at the side of the ring, by the curtain, so that everyone can see it, and so that the music can adapt itself to the performance and the individual artistes.

You can also arrange a rhythm orchestra consisting of pan lids, tambourines, castanets, drums and so on to accompany either a live orchestra or a tape recorder or record player.

If you are using a tape recorder or a record player, it can stand behind the curtain and be operated by someone who can peep out discreetly and keep track of the acts.

If there is a drummer in the orchestra, he can provide a roll of drums to key the audience up to the highest pitch of excitement as they follow some particularly remarkable or difficult detail in one of the acts. It goes without saying that the other members of the orchestra must keep their instruments absolutely quiet at such moments.

Ring, curtain and changing room

Circus is a Latin word and means ring or circle.

The diameter of the ring in a real circus varies somewhat, but it is generally about 45 ft. You cannot, of course, have one as big as that, but you can easily manage with a smaller ring depending on what acts you want to put on. It takes a good deal of space to present a cycling act or a big equestrian act properly.

A ring with a diameter of 16–20 ft. will be quite sufficient in most cases, but you can manage with even less.

The picture on the cover shows how a primitive but good ring can be organized on the lawn; the diameter here was about 10 ft. Twelve posts were used to mark it off, each $1\frac{1}{2}$ in. thick, 22 in. long and pointed at one end. These were set up at a distance of 32 in. apart and driven about 8 in. into the ground, so that they stood about 14 in. high. They were painted white with plastic paint, and cord was nailed to the tops, hanging loosely between the posts, and finally a length of rope was stretched tightly on top. If you like, you can twist a coloured plastic cord round the loose-hanging cord.

The triangle is an ancient jugglers' instrument with many possibilities. It is made of a piece of steel tubing about $\frac{1}{4}$ in. thick with another piece to strike it with. Ready-made triangles can be bought in music shops. The musician plays the instrument by either striking time from outside or allowing the stick to run round inside to a suitable rhythm.

Remember to leave an entrance by the curtain, so that the performers will not fall over getting in and out of the ring.

This method cannot be used on a paved or asphalt playground. In this case the ring will have to be made of cardboard, wooden or plastic boxes all the same size, which can be decorated. If you are using cardboard boxes, you will probably have to put a brick or something heavy in them, to prevent them blowing away.

It is not necessary to paint the whole of the boxes. It will be effective enough to decorate them with large geometric patterns such as triangles, squares or circles. The ring round the ring is known in circus language as the *piste*.

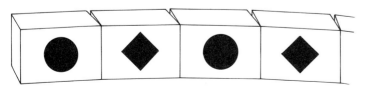

Ring boxes (the piste) *can be decorated on both sides with simple patterns. These can be painted on cardboard boxes with distemper.*

29

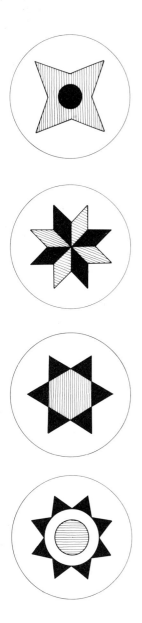

The audience is arranged in rows round the ring on packing cases, chairs or benches.

A curtain is hung behind the ring. This can be just a couple of pieces of sacking decorated with painted clowns' faces, a horseshoe, or perhaps a rearing horse or other circus motifs. To paint on ordinary linen or sacking, soak it in water first; you will then be able to paint on it in oil or plastic paint, and without the risk that the fabric will stiffen and the paint break away when it dries. Instead of a painted curtain, you can perfectly well use a pair of large woollen blankets.

The curtain can, for example, be hung over a clothes-horse.

Behind the curtain you need a 'dressing-room', with a packing-case that will serve as a dressing table, and a mirror.

It is possible that for some of the acts you may have to spread out a quilt for the acrobats or lay a wooden board in the ring. If you can get hold of an old door or possibly two, that will be fine.

It is always said that there has to be sawdust in a circus ring, but for practical reasons we had better ignore that, as it might not be easy to get hold of as much as would be needed, and it makes a mess on a lawn or playground and on a windy day can be quite a nuisance to performers and audience.

If, you are having your circus somewhere where sawdust can be used, however, you can make patterns with coloured sawdust (see p. 22).

See also p. 22 for how to paint with aniline dyes in a ring on a cement floor.

There must be an air of festivity about a circus right from the word go. Put up a couple of flags at the entrance to the ground where it is to be held, and a couple more at the entrance to the circus where the tickets are checked.

Various star designs suitable for decorating a ring.

Dress rehearsal

It is now nearly time for the actual performance, and a few days before that there must be a rehearsal with all the acts run through in the proposed order. The artistes must wear their proper costumes as though it were a real performance.

Just as in a theatre, this is called a dress rehearsal.

Even though everyone may have been very conscientious in working things out and in training you will probably find that there are quite a lot of things that have to be put right before you are ready for an audience.

The ring-master should have followed each of the artistes all the time they were training, so that he knows their acts. At the dress rehearsal he must put the programme into its final shape, as it will be on the day of the real performance.

And he will undoubtedly ask to have the dress rehearsal repeated, if he is not completely satisfied with the result.

For the performers and the rest of the personnel there is only one thing they need do during these rehearsals: do their best and not sulk!

There is only one golden rule, and that is to start with a really good warming-up act so as to get the circus atmosphere going right away.

The rest of the acts must be arranged so as to follow one after the other naturally, and in the most practical way with regard to the apparatus.

Don't let two rather weak acts come one after the other. If there is one particular act that needs complicated apparatus, it is a good idea to use the interval in the middle of the performance for setting this up. If the same performers take part in a number of acts, these should not be allowed to follow one another immediately.

The last act must be one of the best, so that the audience go home with the feeling of really having had value for money.

Circus hands

It is possible that some circus hands will appear at the dress rehearsal for the first time. These are girls or boys who have chosen the important job of lending a hand both in front of the curtain and back stage. They can also help in other ways.

They should be dressed more or less uniformly and hold themselves in readiness to leap forward at the slightest sign from the ring-master or the performers.

When they are not in action, they should stand in a row at the entrance to the ring beside the curtain with their hands behind their backs.

It doesn't look good for either them or the artistes to stand chatting to each other or chewing gum.

Circus hands (centre) with some of the artistes during a rehearsal.

Compère

Large circuses always have a compère. It is his job to say a few words about each individual act and to build up to it so that he kindles the interest of the audience in the performer who is about to appear.

This is in itself a difficult task, but he must also be prepared to take part in a clown's act as the stooge or even possibly to take over the white clown's act, if there isn't one available.

The compère must be dressed for the part. If it is a boy, he could wear a red shirt and long black trousers. If it is a girl, she could have a red blouse and black skirt. The audience must realize, as soon as they see the compère, who he is.

First night

You can start the day with a parade through the neighbour-hood.

All those taking part should put on their costumes and line up. If you can get hold of a wheelbarrow or something of the sort, that will be marvellous. You can also use cycles and prams decorated with balloons. It is a good idea to carry a large placard on a pole in the procession. This will announce yet again that here is an opportunity to see the best circus in Europe.

The whole troupe, with the ring-master at the head, parades through the street to arouse interest in the performance. The posters announce when the performance will take place and give details of some of the acts.

The ring-master walks in solitary state a few paces in front, and the procession marches a few times round the neighbourhood to the sound of music.

You want to be quite sure that everyone has seen or heard you.

In good time before the performance begins the box office attendant sits down at a little table or a packing case at the entrance to the ground or garden.

The flags are hoisted. The public streams in. The weather is marvellous.

The circus begins the moment the public buys the first ticket. A couple of circus hands stand at the entrance to tear the tickets in half.

Over by the ring the audience are received by some of the personnel with the ring-master at the head. He greets the audience and sees that everything is as it should be, while the artistes and the circus hands show people to their seats.

Just before the performance is due to begin the ring-master and all the performers – apart from a couple of circus hands – withdraw behind the curtain.

Two minutes before time the ring-master sounds a loud blast on the whistle as a signal to personnel and audience to be ready. After another minute he sounds another blast.

The third and last blast comes one minute later, and is the signal for the performance to begin. Instead of using a whistle, the ring-master can also ring a bell three times loudly or beat a gong.

Immediately after the third signal the two circus hands draw the curtain aside. The ring-master enters with his whip and advances rapidly to the centre of the ring.

He bows to the audience and says something like:

Ladies and gentlemen,
I have the honour of
welcoming you to our circus.
We hope that you will spend
a couple of pleasant and enjoyable hours
in the company of our excellent artistes
and highly trained animals, so that you will
be able to carry away with you memories
of a real experience.
Once more, I bid you warmly welcome.

The ring master bows, the audience claps. He goes on:

Now I have the pleasure
of presenting to you:
the most beautiful thoroughbred horses in Europe,
imported direct from
the Hungarian steppe.

The circus hands draw the curtain aside again, and the horses run in in a long line.

After presenting the equestrian act, the ring-master bows to the audience. When the applause has died down, he or the compère presents the next number on the programme, and the acts follow on one after the other.

It is irritating for both performers and audience when applause comes at the wrong time. In general, the audience should signal its approval only at the end of an act, or if an artiste gives a definite sign to the audience during the execution of a difficult feat.

In the real theatre or circus they sometimes have 'cheer-leaders' seated at the back of the audience, to start the applause and raise the temperature a few degrees both in front of and behind the curtain.

To make sure that all the performers in your circus get their proper share of applause, regardless of how the act may turn out, it might possibly be a good idea to issue a few free tickets to friends who will lead the applause and take care of that side of the matter.

Half-way through the performance there will be a fifteen-minute interval, in which the audience will have the opportunity to buy lemonade and so forth.

They are also invited for a small extra fee to visit the 'menagerie', which is right at the back. Here the performers and their friends have arranged an exhibition of pets such as white mice, rabbits, bantams, pigeons, dogs, cats or birds.

The second half of the performance sweeps through the ring. Success is yours.

After the last act comes the finale.

All the performers now enter the ring in their costumes, and there are countless ways of organizing a festive final parade or finale.

Final parade at the Circus Zoo,
Nykøbing Falster, where the
manager of the ground, Jacob
Hansen, ran a children's circus
from 1951 to 1957.

The personnel can now:

1. Place themselves on the steps of a ladder set up sideways in the centre of the ring. They hold on with one hand, facing front, waving with their free hand as they receive the plaudits of the audience. The ring-master stands in front of the ladder, facing the audience, and thanks them for coming. Everyone stands smiling and waving down from the ladder to the audience.

2. Space themselves out round the outside of the ring, turning alternately left and right as they enter the ring in procession. The ring-master stands either flanked by the performers in the *piste,* or in the centre of the ring itself.

3. Place themselves in a row right across the ring with the ring-master in front.

In the last two cases the finale can be made still more festive by everyone holding a little paper flag.

At every circus première there are flowers at the end of the performance.

The ring-master sees to it in advance that there is a small bouquet with greetings and thanks from him to all the artistes – and a bouquet for himself. If you have the chance to pick a few flowers beforehand, it is the circus hands' job to hand out these bouquets during the finale.

Apart from that, it is up to the audience to present a small bouquet to individual artistes. These bouquets can be presented either by one of the circus hands or by the donor himself.

It will certainly not be taken amiss if the gracious donor prefers to present the circus company with a basket of fruit or other edibles for distribution rather than flowers. This can be handed to the ring-master or distributed at once.

The ring-master's last job is to thank the audience, which can of course be done in many ways, as for example:

> '*Ladies and gentlemen,*
> *that is the end of our performance.*
> *We thank you for coming, and hope you have enjoyed your-*
> *selves.*
> *If you have been pleased,*
> *tell your friends and acquaintances.*
> *If you have not been pleased, tell me,*
> *and I promise not to tell anyone.*
> *Goodbye, goodbye, and a safe journey home!*'

Circus Acts

I am now going to consider some of the acts you can perform yourselves. Possibly you already know acts which are not included in this book – in that case, all you have to do is to remember them.

It is not my purpose here to explain how to turn a somersault, do a headspring, a handspring, or walk on your hands.

Some of the acts are described in some detail, others are merely indicated, so that you can work further on them yourselves. Several were easier to illustrate with a drawing or a photograph rather than giving a long explanation.

Here is a list of some of the main groups of circus disciplines. They will be followed by a fuller explanation of how to set about doing them.

Acrobatics	Dogs	Trapeze and rings
Balancing acts	Juggling acts	Conjuring
Cowboy acts	Clowns	Weight-lifting
Dancing	Trick cyclists	
Equestrian acts	Tightrope walking	

Now straight on to the first group.

Acrobatics

Somersaults, headsprings, handsprings, handstands, walking on your hands, forming a bridge and doing the splits. These are just a few things you can do if you are good at gymnastics.

And here is a combination: stand on your hands, swing your legs backwards and form a bridge. From this position raise your legs up again. Stand on your hands again and proceed at an easy tempo.

Here is a difficult act. Lie on your stomach. Sway your back as hard as you can and bend one leg up towards your head and draw the other right up with your hand, so that the tips of your toes touch your hair. Hold that position a moment and smile at the audience. Shift to the other leg and smile.

And an easier one. Grasp your ankles with your hands and

A troupe of acrobats uniformly dressed. It is important that all movements are made to time. If this is adhered to, what you do need not be so difficult. It will look good anyway.

bend right down keeping your legs straight, until your forehead touches your knees. Turn your head and smile at the audience.

It will look good if you can arrange some of the numbers on a good strong table.

Acrobatic acts are more effective if you can produce a whole troupe rather than just one or two acrobats.

With training you can learn to pick up a scarf or a flower with your mouth when you make a bridge.

You can crawl through a ring 16–20 in. in diameter in various ways. Here are two:
1. First one leg, then one arm, then the head, then the other arm. The ring will now fall off the other leg.
2. Put both feet inside the ring and squat down. Then stick your arms and head through. Press the ring down over your crouching body, and it will slide off at the back.

Acrobatics at the Circus Zoo, Nykøbing Falster.

Pyramid building

The way to build a pyramid is best shown with the help of illustrations.

Top left: *artists from the Ping Club build a pyramid on the open air stage in the Tivoli, Copenhagen.*

Top right: *pyramid builders from the Ping Club appearing with the Schumann Circus in Fyns Forum, Odense.*

Bottom: *Chinese pyramid builders from Odense.*

41

Comic acrobatics

Four or five performers pull their hair down over their faces and put a mask on the back of their necks. If your hair is too short, put on a hat with long artificial hair that can hang down and cover your face (see p. 25). Girls wear artificial busts on their backs (see p. 18). Clothes are put on back to front.

The acrobats stand in a row in front of the curtain and execute the most fantastic acts, which would otherwise take years of training. But the tempo must be kept perfect. The acrobats can bend backwards with the utmost ease and do other neck-breaking things. The troupe concludes the act by going down on all fours and marching out in time to the music.

It is a good idea to set up a board or something of the sort in front of the acrobats, so that the audience cannot see that the toes of their shoes are pointing the wrong way!

Four young acrobats from the Ping Club leave the Schumann Circus ring in Fyns Forum, Odense, in this elegant manner.

Balancing acts

Rolling barrels

You can roll into the ring on a barrel (for instance an oil barrel) and roll it backwards and forwards. You might at the same time play with a couple of balls.

It can be difficult to control an empty barrel, but if it is filled a quarter full with water, it is easier to work with.

Walking on stilts

Stilts must be a good 6 ft. high. They are made of pinewood, $1\frac{1}{2} \times 2\frac{1}{2}$ in. There must not be more than two steps on each stilt, never three, as you can hurt yourself very badly falling off (see fig.).

A stilt act can look very comical if a pair of old, flat shoes are stuck under the stilts.

Here are a few stilt numbers:

1. You can walk over a circus hand or a clown sitting on a stool in the ring.
2. Standing on the bottom step you can walk over brightly painted cardboard boxes or something of the sort, set in a row at suitable intervals. For safety reasons *never* walk over children, as it can be very dangerous to be trodden on with a stilt.
3. You can take very long steps on stilts. This looks funny.
4. If one artiste stands on the bottom step of the stilts, another can sit on his shoulders. The one on top gets up by means of a ladder or a tall box. If the one below is strong, he can work himself up on to the top step with the other one on his back.
5. You can jump on a stilt, though this is not very easy. The act can be combined, so that two artistes encounter each other, each on a stilt. In the end one of them gets both stilts.

You can have a black bandage over your eyes. A suitable material is tarlatan, which is very loosely woven. You can see through it quite clearly, if it is a single thickness.

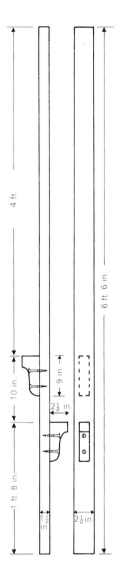

How to make a pair of stilts.

43

Chinese plate act

A hole about $\frac{1}{8}$ in. in diameter is bored right at the edge of an earthenware or plastic plate. A headless nail is driven into one end of a stick about 20 in. long, so that it sticks out about $\frac{1}{2}$ in. You enter the ring with the stick in one hand and the plate in the other, bow to the audience and fix the plate over the stick, with the nail passing through the hole. The audience must not, of course, see this little trick, which professional artistes would never dream of using. At the same time you set the plate spinning rapidly round and work on through the act with the help of the stick. At the end of the act, throw the plate lightly up into the air, catch it, bow to the audience and run off.

Many circus disciplines can be combined. Here is a skilful acrobat-cum-plate performer. The act is a variation on that described in the text, as here the stick is applied to the centre of the plate. The plate will therefore require an occasional push with the hand, to keep it spinning round and maintain its balance.

As it is not possible to bore holes in porcelain (it is too hard) you have to be able to tell the difference between porcelain and earthenware, which is very easy to bore through with an ordinary metal borer.

Hold a plate up to the light and move the other hand up and down between the plate and the light. If you can see the shadow of your hand through the plate, it is porcelain, if not, it is earthenware.

Comic balancing act

You will need a narrow broomstick about $2\frac{1}{2}$ ft. long. Nail a cork on at one end which fits a dark bottle, perhaps a beer bottle. Fix the bottle over the cork. The performer enters the ring balancing the bottle upside down at the very end of the

Balancing stick with trick cork.

45

The tray is screwed to the top of the broomstick. Bore a hole first – so as not to split the wood. The tray may be round or square as preferred.

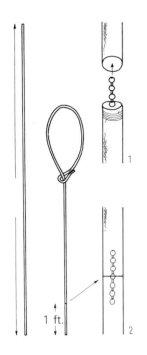

Lasso with concealed chain.

broomstick. He makes it look, of course, as though it was very difficult. Suddenly he discovers that he has to hurry off, or the ring-master calls him off. He completely loses his head and puts the broomstick over his shoulder, with the bottle hanging down, and runs out.

The act can also be worked with a long carrot, preferably with its top on, stuck to a nail at the end of the broomstick.

You can do a similar act with a couple of glasses – provided they have relatively flat bottoms, so that there is something to stick on to – stuck on with Araldite to a small wooden tray, which can be home-made. The tray is then screwed on to the end of a broomstick. The act is presented like the preceding one, except that here, of course, the broomstick has to be held vertically while it is being displayed. With a little practice you can learn to balance the apparatus on your forehead or chin.

Cowboy acts

Whirling a lasso

A lasso is made of a woven cotton rope $\frac{3}{8}$–$\frac{1}{2}$ in. thick and about $4\frac{1}{2}$ yds. long. This can be bought in shops that sell marine stores and ropes.

Make a loop big enough for the rope to slide through easily. Cut off a piece about 1 ft. long from the other end. This piece is attached to the lasso again with either a short piece of chain (such as is used, among other things, for attaching plugs in hand basins) which can be bought at a shop that sells domestic hardware or an ironmonger's, or better still, a small swivel, which can be bought at a shop that sells fishing tackle. These small joints are not visible to the audience and they prevent the lasso from tangling. Professional artistes would never use these sort of tricks, but it is necessary here, as it takes a very long time to learn to do a proper lasso act.

The difficult part about whirling a lasso is to get started, but with a little practice it comes. You can start in various ways:

1. Start the 'wheel' or loop of the lasso spinning with your free hand and at the same time make a rotating movement in the same direction with the hand that holds the 'handle' of the lasso.

Søren Aggi of Brabrand swinging a lasso.

47

2. The lasso can be laid in a wide circle on the ground in front of the performer and be started off from here with an even rotating movement of the 'handle'.
3. Finally you can start with the loop round the artiste's body. Move the 'handle' with a rapid rotating movement, at the same time flinging the body round and steering the loop with the other hand. In the photograph Søren Aggi shows how elegant the result can be.

If the lasso gives a lot of trouble at the start, try reversing the loop in relation to the 'handle'.

Sharp-shooting

For this you need a toy pistol with quite a loud report. Also a screen with two upright sides, such as the bottom and sides of a very large cardboard box. Set up the screen right in front of the curtain. In the top quarter of the side that is turned towards the audience cut three holes side by side. These should be slightly smaller than a blown-up balloon. Before carrying in the screen, blow up three differently coloured balloons and fix them in the holes. The act goes as follows: one of the circus hands crawls out from behind the curtain and conceals himself behind the screen. The ring-master praises the phenomenal skill of the marksman and the marksman explodes the balloons one after the other. This is done quite simply by the circus hand who is sitting hidden behind the screen, sticking a pin into the balloons in the correct order. Remember that it must be the correct order! That is why the balloons are all different colours, so that the ring-master can tell the marksman distinctly which balloon to hit.

You can also have a little Red Indian girl standing in front of the screen with her arms raised slightly. She looks, of course, as though she has a balloon in each hand and also one above her head. The two she has in her hands are burst first, and then the one over her head.

The circus hand must make sure that the audience cannot see him through the holes in the screen as the balloons are burst.

The marksman can make the number more exciting. He can turn his back on the screen and aim over one shoulder with the aid of a small pocket mirror which he holds up in front of him. Or he can bend down with his back to the screen and shoot between his legs.

Professional artistes never, of course, cheat with pins and so forth. They are really fine marksmen who have gained their skill through years of training.

In acts in which a great deal is made of the costumes, as in this case, where the marksman perhaps has a cowboy hat on and is dressed as a cowboy, the musical accompaniment can further heighten the atmosphere. It would be marvellous, for example, to play a record of a couple of cowboy or Western songs.

Parodies of sharp shooting
You can also parody a sharp-shooting act.

A clown comes into the ring swinging a rifle or large pistol made of wood. He crashes around and finally settles himself in front of the target, takes aim very carefully a number of times and finally pulls the trigger. But instead of the loud report the audience has been expecting, a strip of material unrolls from the pistol, bearing the word 'BANG!'. The clown is driven off by the ring-master.

The rifle or pistol can be made of a round piece of wood as the barrel and a sawn-off lump as the butt. The trigger can be a nail, and the guard around it can be made of tin. The word 'BANG' is painted on linen or canvas with a rod at the bottom to give it weight. The linen is pinned to the barrel. It is rolled up round the rod and held in place by a piece of string, which is wound round the barrel a few times and made fast with a loop round the trigger. To shoot you loosen the loop.

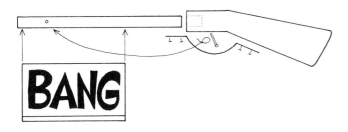

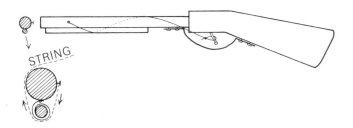

The rifle butt is sawn out and a hole bored for the barrel.

49

Finally, you can scrap the 'serious' sharp-shooting act altogether and substitute the following clowning act, for the two acts cannot be included in the same programme.

The act will go exactly as described on p. 48, but now the marksman is more self-important and superior.

He and the ring-master have not noticed that it is the clown who is sitting behind the screen, but the audience has, for when the marksman and the ring-master turn their backs to the screen, the clown jumps out and makes faces and shows the audience a large darning needle.

The ring-master points out which coloured balloon to burst. The marksman takes careful aim and pulls the trigger,

In this Indian act the snake-charmer by his flute-playing gets the snake to rise up out of the basket and move in time to the music, while a veil dancer may perform on one side. The music can be provided by a record. A silken thread or a piece of nylon fishing line is tied to the snake's neck, and runs through an eyelet hole on the flute to the musician's little finger. As he moves his hand, the snake rises and sinks. The snake can be made of material or of a piece cut from a cycle tyre. Or you could buy one at a toy shop. The snake in the photograph on the right moves by means of a piece of strong steel wire, which is passed through the side of the basket, so that the snake charmer can move the snake from outside. The two snake acts are from the Circus Zoo, Odense.

but after a slight pause the *wrong* balloon bursts.

The ring-master abuses the marksman while the clown peeps out through the hole in the screen and waves to the audience.

The same thing happens again with the next shot, but with the balloon bursts *before* the shot is fired.

The ring-master drives the marksman off, while the clown waves through the last hole.

Dancing

There are many kinds of dancing and some are exactly right for the circus. It is impossible to describe all the different kinds here, so I will just list some of the possibilities, say a word about costumes and give a few tips.

Ballet dancing, veil dancing, tap dancing, Spanish dancing with a tambourine or castanets, dancing on roller skates and Hawaiian dancing with hulahoop rings are some of the possibilities to choose from.

Here you can really make your own costumes.

A dress for a veil dance need not be expensive. It can be made, for example, of light red crêpe paper, and the dancer can wear a bow in her hair to match. The thin veil is attached to her middle finger with a small loop. During the dance the

Bare-legged Hawaiian dancers. The skirt is made of raffia. The garlands of flowers, which also serve as bras, are made of scraps of coloured material.

51

Butterfly dance performed by girls from the Ping Club in the Schumann Circus, Fyns Forum, Odense.

veil is flung in graceful folds in front, to the sides and behind, and the dancer leaves the ring with small, tripping steps and with the veil fluttering from side to side. The veil dance is eminently suitable for pair dancing.

Hulahoop dancing

Hulahoop rings can usually be bought in toy shops, particularly at times when they are fashionable. You could also make one. The diameter of the ring is about 2 ft. 6 in. You need a piece of $\frac{3}{4}$ in. plastic hose pipe with a strong steel wire run through it. The steel wire is welded together, bringing the ends of the hose pipe as close together as possible. The gap is covered over with insulating tape.

The costume for dancing with a hulahoop ring is, of course, a raffia skirt, a bra and a garland of flowers round the neck. A Hawaiian girl is dark-haired with a light brown skin.

Tap dancing

Tap dancing can be done on a wooden board, or even an old door, which is laid down in the ring. The dancer need not wear proper tap dancing shoes, for if she is not expert at tap dancing, one of the circus hands can produce the sounds from behind the scenes by banging on a table or a wooden packing case with a couple of pieces of wood, while discreetly following the dance through a hole in the curtain!

Dancing doll

The dancing rag doll is made from a pair of old tights, stuffed with newspaper or corrugated paper in the legs and rags in the feet. The tops can be stitched to a large flat cardboard box which represents the body. Cover this with a dress with long sleeves and if necessary stuff it with cushions. The arms can be made of stuffed lady's stockings, ending in a pair of stuffed

An act with hulahoop rings. The performers all wear similar trousers.

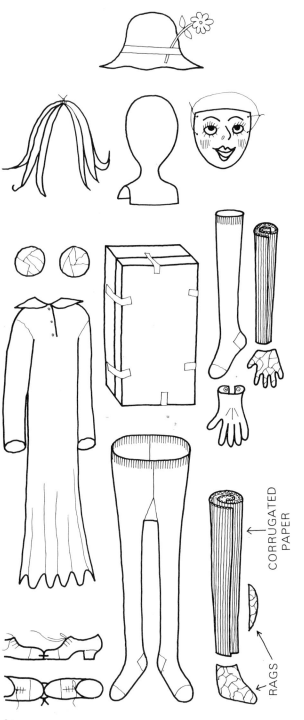

The various parts of a dancing doll. The lady's and gentleman's shoes are sewn tightly together with, for example, string. The ends are tied in a strong knot on the outside, as shown in the bottom left drawing.

CORRUGATED PAPER

RAGS

The dancing doll follows her partner's movements through thick and thin. If he is got up in a mask or a false nose, the effect is funnier.

gloves. The basic shape of the head can be made of papier mâché or 'gauze mâché' over a balloon according to the instructions give on p. 26. The features can be shaped in the gauze or the doll can wear a lady's mask. It doesn't matter if she looks a little stupid. The hair can be made of twist, glued on to the head with artificial resin glue. The doll can be finished off with a scarf over the head or a lady's hat. It is very important for the shoes to be firmly fixed to the feet. Use canvas shoes if possible, which can be stitched on with strong linen thread or possibly thin string; if necessary, use upholsterer's pins. The toecaps of the lady's shoes are firmly attached to the toecaps of the man's shoes, which should also, if possible, be of canvas (see drawing).

It is quite fantastic how that couple can dance! The lady is suppleness itself! She twists and turns and can bend backwards amazingly. It all looks completely ridiculous, especially if the act follows a solemn veil dance.

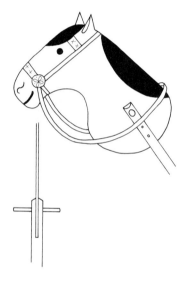

Equestrian acts

No circus is complete without horses!

But of course you cannot have real horses in your little ring. So you must make them yourselves, either in the form of hobby-horses, theatrical horses or pantomime horses.

A hobby-horse can be made in various ways, but here is quite an easy one. This is the one to use if you have to make a number of horses for a big equestrian act.

Hobby-horse's head. A circus horse must always look pleasant, and must never show its teeth. The little drawing on the left shows the crossbar used to steer the horse. This passes through both neck and stick. The length of the stick naturally depends on the size of the rider, so this is a thing you will have to decide for yourselves.

Ordinary hobby-horse

The horse's head is cut out of a piece of strong cardboard or, better still, sawn out of a piece of masonite with a fretsaw, after first making a pattern to draw the head from. The horse's head is set firmly on a broomstick in which a groove has been sawn of the right thickness to take it.

Two nails must be driven in. Bore the holes first with a bradawl, so as not to split the wood.

Nail a piece of string on each side of the mouth as a rein.

The horses can be painted white, black or brown, but it is best to divide the colours equally among the total number of horses to be shown in the ring.

Hobby-horse with a shaped head

Horses can be made more lifelike with a head shaped of papier mâché, or with a head and neck made from a man's old sock stuffed with rags. The head must have the ears sewn on. It is tied on to a broomstick and provided with reins. If the colour of the sock is not suitable, it can be dyed with fabric dye, for instance a strong batik dye, or painted with plastic paint. The eyes can also be painted or a couple of buttons sewn on. It is quite a complicated business to make this horse, so use it only for very special solo acts.

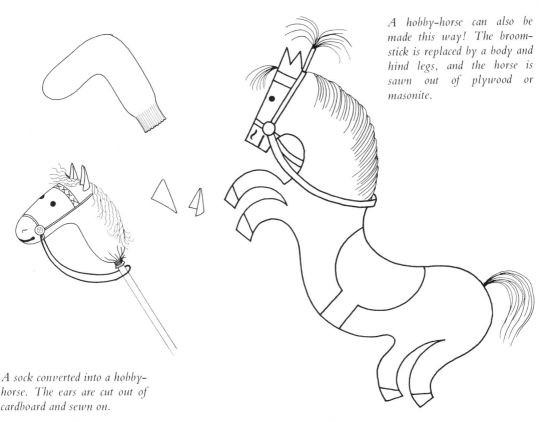

A hobby-horse can also be made this way! The broomstick is replaced by a body and hind legs, and the horse is sawn out of plywood or masonite.

A sock converted into a hobby-horse. The ears are cut out of cardboard and sewn on.

Hobby-horse rider with a horse's tail.

The hobby-horse riders should be more or less similarly dressed. They could wear similar shirts and blue military caps made of folded paper, so that they look like hussars.

It is not possible to put a tail on a hobby-horse, but it makes an amusing effect if the rider wears a tail himself. This can be made of 12–16 in. of unravelled sacking. The threads are gathered together over a piece of bent steel wire, which is stuck into the back of the performer's belt, or possibly down his trousers. The wire is shaped so that the first part of the tail stands up in the air a little and looks like a real horse's tail.

Here is a theatrical horse. It is not exactly easy to make, but it looks good in the ring.

A loop made of steel wire is stuck in at the back of the belt. The tail, which can be made of an unravelled sack, is twisted firmly round the wire.

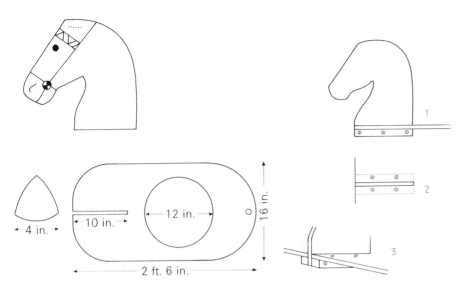

Theatrical horse

A theatrical horse is made as shown in the drawing. You can also make a bull in the same way with a papier mâché head, or the head can be sawn out of a piece of expanded polystyrene. You can put on a comic bull-fighting act with a toreador mounted on a horse, in which the bull wins in fine style and chases the horse out, bellowing loudly.

Riding

And now to the act itself.

The ring-master brings in the horses. They run into the ring in a line. When they run round, it is usually in an anti-clockwise direction. They can also run in a figure-of-eight or a four-leaved clover as shown in the drawings.

The acts can be varied and combined in different ways.

The kind of act in which the ring-master cracks his whip loudly but without touching the horses is known as 'liberty dressage'. A good ring-master never shouts at his horse. He says the horse's name and gives it an order in a low voice, and the horse obeys, if everything goes as planned.

At the end the horses leave the ring either by running out all together, or by the horse at the back turning round on itself anti-clockwise – just beside the exit and running off.

This is how to make a theatrical horse:

The material can be strong cardboard, plywood or masonite. The big hole is cut out with a compass saw. The little curved triangle on the left of the diagram is the pattern for the horse's ears. If the horse is found to tip over forwards while working in the ring, this can be offset by fixing something heavy under the board by the tail. Finally a piece of (preferably brightly coloured) material is thrown over the whole 'body'. You can also paint the head and back in a plain colour and fix a 'curtain' round as a horse cloth or caparison.

If you saw the head out of polystyrene (this is done most easily with a loose saw blade), you must put a layer of papier mâché over it afterwards, as the material crumbles very easily. You then paint on to the papier mâché.

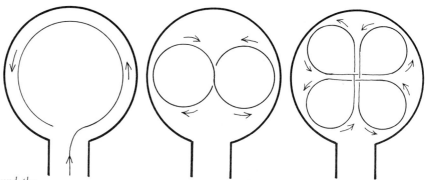

The horses can run round the ring in various ways. They usually run anti-clockwise.

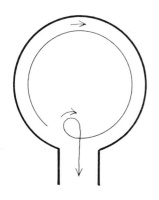

How the horses leave the ring individually.

In this way each time the horses run round there is one horse fewer, until in the end the ring-master only has one horse left.

This is usually a particularly clever horse, which can kneel and walk on its hind legs and so forth. It is rewarded once or twice with a lump of sugar. In the end they leave the ring, the horse going out backwards, while the ring-master holds his whip high above his head.

Jumping horses

The circus hands stand in the ring each holding a pole, which lies horizontally on the edge of the piste. The horses run round the ring and jump over the poles as they come to them. They jump over a couple of times before the poles are removed. There are usually two or four white-painted poles.

The circus hands each hold a pole up against the side of the ring, so that the horses can jump over it. The poles look festive if they are painted red and white.

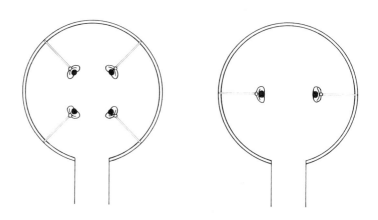

The pantomime horse

Some of you may have seen this act at a circus. It involves putting two people into a 'horse skin' made of material, after which they pretend to be a horse.

The 'horse skin', or in this case rather the horse blanket or caparison, can be made in various ways, some more complicated than others. The simplest is to fold a large piece of sacking or a large plain blanket down the middle. Sew it completely together at one end, which will form the back, and at the other end leave a suitable-sized hole for the head by omitting to sew it together right up to the fold.

A tail made of an unravelled sack can, if you like, be sewn on at the back, and the same material can also be used to make a mane.

The head can be made of papier mâché over chicken netting with a shoe-box or something of the sort as a base.

The sacking or blanket for the horse is folded once. It is sewn together at the front, leaving an opening beside the fold for the artiste's and horse's head. The back is sewn up completely. The dotted lines show where it should be sewn.

The horse's head is made of papier mâché or 'gauze mâché' over a piece of chicken netting or such like, which is shaped roughly like a horse's head. Lay the papier mâché over this and finally make a mane of wool and paint the head with poster colours. You may need to prick holes in the face so as to be able to see out, as there can be no guarantee that the horse's eyes will be at the right angle for one's own head.

61

The two performers, one bigger and one smaller, stand with the smaller one in front. The one behind bends forward and with outstretched arms holds on to the belt of the one in front. They should both if possible wear long trousers of the same colour and the same material.

Now the cover is laid over them, and the man in front puts his head out through the hole and up into the horse's head, which he can support with his hands.

If it is difficult to cover over the join between the neck and the head, a large scarf can be wound round, so that the horse represents a horse with a cold, as the compère will explain.

The pantomime horse can do almost anything a real horse can do – and also a good deal more. It can kick with all four legs. If the edge of the ring is made of wooden packing cases, it can walk quite correctly with its front legs up on these and its back legs down in the ring. But it can also walk the other way round, with its back legs up on the edge and its front legs down in the ring. At the request of the audience it can do sums, both addition and subtraction. It counts by scraping one of its front legs on the ground or standing with its forelegs on an upturned packing case and stamping on it with one foot. It can also answer questions by nodding its head if something is correct or shaking its head if it is wrong. It can do all sorts of things, but it cannot jump over the poles held up by the circus hands against the wall of the piste. But this must not prevent the ring-master from ordering it to jump, because it looks so funny. The horse seems to get tired, or is apparently unable to take any more, for it suddenly stands stock still in the centre of the ring with its fore or hind legs crossed, or with both fore and hind legs crossed. It may sit down or lie down, or it may dance to classical music. The ring-master has a terrible job to get it to put its forelegs up on a pedestal, a packing case standing upside down in the ring. The horse misunderstands, and puts either both its hind legs up or just one of them. In the end it lands up by mistake with all four legs up on the little pedestal, so that it turns into a tall, hunchbacked horse. Or it may kneel down and kick the ring-master on the behind, if he gets too insistent, and in the end the horse chases the ring-master round. He gives up and runs out of the ring with the crazy horse after him.

It would take too long to put the horse through all its paces in one act, but it is always possible to divide them up into two acts, one before the interval and one after. Alternatively, it is not absolutely necessary to show them all.

A rider would like to get up on to the horse's back, but it is not exactly easy to handle! The photograph shows the Benneweis Circus, Copenhagen, with artistes from the Ping Club.

Bottom left:

A 'skin' for a horse or a wild animal can be made of linen sheeting or thin sackcloth. The head is made of papier mâché or 'gauze mâché'. Here is a splendid tiger!

A kind tiger, too!

Dogs

If anyone has a dog that can do tricks, it is quite in order to have him in the programme.

But I would like to warn you seriously against trying to train a dog or any other animal just because you want to produce a circus.

Leave the training of animals severely alone. It needs to be done by professional trainers, who work according to the principles of animal psychology, which do not harm the animal and which take the trainer a long time to learn.

However if someone has a dog that knows a trick, then let it join in the performance, but only if it does not mind, and if its owner shows it.

The act could consist of the dog sitting up nicely with a piece of sugar on its nose, dancing round after a titbit, and at the end saying goodbye by giving a paw.

A dog can look like a funny little horse if it has a saddle of material or cardboard tied to its back and a doll as rider.

But do not attempt to make a little horse's head of papier mâché to put on the dog's head. A normal dog will not wear a mask. You may have seen an act like that at a real circus, but that is the result of years of training beginning when the dog was a puppy, so that it knows the mask and knows that it is nothing to be frightened of.

See also 'The strong dog' in the section about the interval clown on p. 68.

Juggling acts

A real juggling act is difficult and takes years of training. The only thing of this sort possible here is playing with balls. And perhaps the girls will be best at that!

Many girls can play with two balls, and some master the art of playing three. Four is extremely rare.

It is easiest to keep control with heavy balls the size of a tennis ball.

Clowns

There are many kinds of clowns, and it will not be possible to mention all the different types.

Types of clown

The most usual is the August clown or vagabond clown. He may wear clothes that are too big for him, a jacket inside out and great clumsy shoes that he keeps falling about in. He may wear a padlock on his stomach or a huge safety pin to keep his jacket together, an alarm clock, a large bottle-opener, an out-size baby's dummy or an enormous comb.

An August clown shouts and makes a great to-do if he gets chaffed or everything does not go exactly to his liking.

Another type very reminiscent of the August clown is Stupid Peter. As his name indicates, he is a pretty poor specimen too. He appears in a number of the traditional clown entrées given in this book, but here we merely call him Peter, as it is not his fault that he is not very clever.

The white clown wears a pointed hat and a fine costume, often imaginatively decorated and very colourful. He is known as the white clown because his face is made up to look white. He always has red ears and red lips and usually one or two black streaks on his forehead. Each clown has his own way of drawing these streaks, so that they become the clown's hallmark.

He is one of those superior sort of people who enjoy hectoring others, and naturally he takes it out of August and Peter in the first instance. But it frequently happens that his

Musical clowns in Odense.

The bladder. The bag must be firmly fixed so that it does not fall off. Bore a couple of holes through the stick and sew through these. The stick must not project very far into the bag.

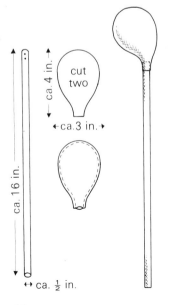

luck turns and the white clown is the one who looks small in the end, to the great joy of the audience.

To underline his dignity the white clown carries a bladder, which is an instrument of punishment made of a stick about 16 in. long and about $\frac{1}{2}$ in. thick. It has a small pear-shaped bag of thin wash-leather at the end, about 3 in. wide and 4 in. long, filled with down. Don't use kapok or anything like that, as it would hurt too much.

He uses the bladder to hit the other clowns with when he loses patience with them, or strikes his own hand with it when he wants to give weight to his words.

In large circuses it is often the white clown who plays against the August clown. For practical reasons we can often let the compère or the ring-master take the part of the white

66

clown, but you may feel it would be fun to have a proper white clown in the circus, and if you can get the costume made, that is the best solution.

It is very difficult to be a good clown, and quite impossible to tell anyone how to do it.

When the clown enters the ring, it is called a 'clown-entrée,' and when the clown talks to someone else, e.g. the ring-master or another clown, it is called a 'clown-dialogue'.

Different types of clown.

Here is a little practical trick that is used by professional artistes. If you are putting on a clown entrée with dialogue or a long, silent action sequence, as for example in 'The Mirror', keep a little piece of paper in your hand with the cues written on it and take a peep at it every now and then without being seen. This way you will remember to include all the action and will avoid drying up, which can be very uncomfortable.

Something must be going on all the time in a circus performance, even while the circus hands are clearing the ring for the next act.

And this is where the interval clown comes into the picture. He is as a rule the August clown, and it is his job to entertain the audience while the apparatus is being set up or taken down. He does this with a number of short, independent entrées, which fill up the interval.

The interval clown will also often come in and make fun of the act that has just been shown. However it takes a good deal of talent to make fun of another performer's act. Actually the clown has to know the act in every detail and almost be able to do it himself.

But if he has the right apparatus, he can often make fun of a good many numbers. See, for example, the comic balancing act (p. 45), the sharp-shooting parody (p. 49), the dancing doll (p. 53), and tightrope walking (p. 84). All these clown entrées, by the way, are taken from real circus and juggling performances.

Balance

In the chapter on balancing acts there is a description of a Chinese plate act which can be converted into a short clown entrée. The headless nail at the end of the stick is replaced by a nail with such a large head that the plate cannot possibly fall off. The head of the nail is painted white like the plate.

The turn consists of the clown coming into the ring balancing the plate. He then presents a completely fantastic act and at the end puts the stick with the plate hanging from it over his shoulder and marches out.

Here are other examples of entrées suitable for the interval clown.

The strong dog

The clown comes into the ring dragging a very thick, heavy rope. When he is a good way in he stops suddenly because

The interval clown with the little dog on the thick rope. The painted pole he is treading on is one of the poles the hobby-horse riders jump over.

there is a violent jerk on the rope. He starts pulling at it hard and shouting abuse. He hauls away with might and main, but even so he is being pulled out backwards.

At last, when he is on the point of being dragged out through the curtain, it gives way and he sits down violently on the ground. He gets to his feet again and starts pulling on the rope and this time all goes well. Then a tiny little dog appears with the rope tied firmly to its collar. They go once round the ring and out.

The gallant clown

The clown comes in holding a flower so carefully hidden behind his back that everyone sees it. He is very mysterious and casts loving looks at all the ladies in the audience. In the end he decides on one and cautiously approaches her. He now produces the flower and hands it to the lady, who naturally accepts it. The clown withdraws to the ring smiling a knowing smile. The lady finds herself holding the green tube the flower

The clown's trick flower. The bottom part of the stalk is cut smooth and a casing of strong paper is rolled round the stalk and glued together, so that the flower stalk can just pass through. Can be painted the colour of the stalk.

69

was stuck into. The clown then goes off and offers the flower to some other lady among the audience.

The entrée can be done another way, with a bunch of flowers laid loosely on the top of some cut-off stalks with a string round them. The lady will then be left holding a handful of stalks after the clown has delivered the bouquet.

The red elastic

The clown stoops down and picks up something from the ring. He stands examining it and then puts it in his pocket. Then he calls out, 'Who has dropped a bundle of pound notes with an elastic band round them?'

Everyone who happens to be round about, musicians, artistes and circus hands, starts feeling in his pockets and they all shout out together: 'I have, I have!'

The clown: 'Are you quite sure? A bundle like that with a red elastic band round?'

Everyone: 'Yes, yes!'

The clown: 'Well. I've found the elastic!'

The spectacles

The clown cleans his spectacles. Evidently he is not satisfied, for he breathes on them and rubs them carefully with a pocket handkerchief. It takes a long time. At last it appears that there is no glass in the spectacles, for he pushes his handkerchief through the holes and draws it backwards and forwards, holding a corner of it between his teeth.

The dwarf clown

For this you need a strong cardboard box or a wooden box, about 2 ft. × about 16 in. × about 16 in. Paint the bottom, the ends and one side of the box on the outside. Lay it on the ground with the opening at the back. Cut a pair of old shoes in half and stick or nail the front half on top of the box, so that the opening of the shoes is in line with the back of the box. Spread a rug over the box and the shoes and all is ready. Stand the apparatus close up against the curtain.

The act goes as follows: the clown comes in and stands as

near as possible exactly behind the box, so that his trousers are just behind the shoe tops. He whisks off the rug and the audience now behold a dwarf clown, who breaks into some sort of patter.

Four short clown entrées

The interval clown's entrées are characteristically short and simple, so that he can manage them alone.

Here are a few examples of entrées that require the co-operation of other clowns, the compère or the ring-master. This type of entrée is longer and more complicated, and is included on the programme as part of the circus performance.

In the entrées the action and the points are described exactly, but the dialogue is only roughly sketched, so that there is plenty of opportunity to fill out the skeleton with gags and run the entrées together so that the final result is a single unit.

1. 'You have eleven fingers!' 'No!' 'Yes, you have!' He counts 1–2–3–4–5 on one hand and on the other 10–9–8–7–6. 'You can see for yourself, five and six make eleven!'

2. The clown puts a pocket handkerchief under the ring-master's hat on the ground. He says to the ring-master: 'I can take out that pocket handkerchief without touching the hat!' The ring-master protests. They argue backwards and forwards, whether it is possible, and suddenly the clown says, 'The handkerchief has gone now!' The ring-master does not believe it, but he picks up the hat to see whether it is true. The clown immediately snatches up the handkerchief and shouts over and over again, 'Without-touching-the-hat!'

3. The clown shows the ring-master two large figures of three which are cut out of cardboard. 'What do three and three make?' asks the clown. 'Six', replies the ring-master. 'No, they make eight,' cries the clown, holding the two figures of three against each other so as to form an eight.

4. When the clown goes to pick up his hat, he repeatedly kicks it forward with his big shoe. But even a good joke can be overdone, so stop in time! In the end one of the circus hands picks the hat up and hands it to the clown, who says, 'Listen, young man, you don't happen to have five pence?' 'Yes, I think so,' says the circus hand obligingly, and starts feeling in his pocket. He finds the coin at last and hands it to the clown, who waves it away with a magnificent gesture, saying, 'Good! Keep it as a tip.'

Three and three make eight!

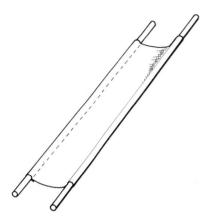

A stretcher can be made of two poles and a piece of sacking. It need not have legs.

Sharp-shooting

This act requires two clowns of the August type (but you can also have one marksman in a different costume or a white clown).

One of the clowns persuades the other, after a great deal of talk, to stand up in the ring and hold a dinner plate over his head as a target. He says that he will smash it to smithereens with a single shot.

The marksman takes aim. All that is heard is the roll of a drum.

The shot rings out, but the plate remains whole. The clown shakes his head, brings the plate down and with many grimaces spits out a bullet on to it, so that everyone can hear it. All the time he is grumbling away that the shot hit him in the mouth instead of hitting the plate.

The marksman tries again, but with the same result.

The third time it is very difficult to persuade the clown, but he agrees.

When the shot is fired, the clown falls down in the ring. He is still holding the plate, with his arms stretched out at his sides and his legs apart.

The marksman calls a circus hand, who comes running up with a stretcher, which he puts on the ground beside the clown. The circus hand goes to the head of the clown lying on the ground, who is now to be lifted on to the stretcher.

The marksman takes hold of his legs and draws them together, but at that moment his arms shoot out so that they are at right angles to his body. The circus hand brings his arms back to his sides, but now his legs shoot out at the same moment. This is repeated a few times, and the entrée ends with the clown lying on the ground suddenly letting out a yell, getting up and spitting a third bullet out on to the plate, after which the marksman and the circus hand are chased off by the ring-master. The bullets can be represented by small stones. Do not on any account use shot, as this can cause lead poisoning.

Elvira the tightrope walker

A clown sits in the centre of the ring watching a piece of string stretched between two pointed sticks, which can easily be stuck into the ground. If the ring is on asphalt, you will have

to set up some sort of stand, like the one shown in the drawing. Underneath the string is a glass of water, from which the clown takes a sip every now and then. He is following with great enjoyment something that is apparently moving slowly backwards and forwards along the string. Another clown comes up and asks what all the excitement is about. 'Look,' says the clown, 'my trained she-flea, Elvira.' He points to it and explains that it is the only flea in the world that is trained to walk a tightrope carrying a parasol. The other clown is very interested, and they sit talking about the skill of the tightrope walker and all that she can do. Suddenly something splashes into the glass of water (actually a small stone, thrown in by one of the clowns). They examine the glass in consternation and announce that Elvira has drowned and a really sensational act has died with her.

The balloon pumps

This is not really a clown entrée but an amusing turn. It can be used either as a separate act on the programme or to replace another that may have fallen through.

The circus hands bring two pedestals or stools into the ring.

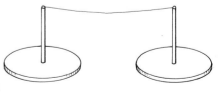

The flea's tightrope.

73

On each is an air pump of the kind used to pump up rubber mattresses. A balloon is attached to the end of the two tubes.

The ring-master or a clown invites two children from the audience to come into the ring and take part in a little competition, for which there is a prize. The competitors must be big enough for their feet to reach the ground when they sit on the stools. They sit on the two pumps holding the tubes in their hands, and the idea is to see which of them gets his balloon pumped up first to the point where it bursts. They have to lift their weight and sit down again on the pump alternately. The prize could be a balloon.

You could dress up the act by giving the participants a funny hat and a red nose.

The mirror

August tells Peter that it is his birthday, and that in honour of the occasion he has bought himself a new suit of clothes and a fine mirror. He asks Peter to bring the mirror into his bedroom, so that he can look at himself in it again and see how smart he looks. Two stools have already been brought into the ring and two bottles of mineral water. August has also been given a bottle of wine for a birthday present. This stands at the edge of the ring, and every now and then he takes a swig. He has reached the talkative stage, and while he stands fooling with the audience, there is a sound of broken glass behind the scenes. (You can buy pieces of metal in joke shops that you strike against a wooden floor or tray and they sound like breaking glass.) A moment later Peter comes in with the frame of a large mirror that stands upright (see photograph). Peter is obviously afraid that August will discover that the mirror is broken, and so he is now made up and dressed exactly the same as August, apart from the fact that their hats are not the same.

August starts walking towards the mirror. He is a little unsteady on his legs, and he is in a good mood.

Peter also starts walking towards the mirror, but from the opposite side of the ring. He walks exactly the same way as August and tries to imitate him in every detail – but in reverse as in a mirror!

The following jokes are only indications of some of the

situations the two clowns can dramatize, and this is an opportunity to create a really good clown entrée.

One little tip to the artistes: remember that August is not absolutely sober, so his movements are fairly slow. This can be a help to the clowns, in that it makes it easier to follow each other's movements. Of course it is August who takes the lead all the time.

August discovers a spot on the mirror. He takes his handkerchief to rub the spot off, but it proves obstinate. He breathes on the spot and rubs harder and it goes.

August looks in the mirror to admire his new suit. Discovers that Peter's hat looks different from his own. Turns to look at the audience in astonishment, but while he is doing so Peter exchanges their hats, so that when August looks in the mirror again, he sees the image he expected. He looks relieved.

August scratches an ear.

August blows his nose.

August scratches his head.

August takes out his purse and starts counting his money. If you want to be really daring, you could let Peter have six coins and August four. Of course they count out loud and cannot make it balance. They count once again, and then Peter gives August a coin, so that they both have five coins.

August tidies his hair.

August sits down on a stool and gazes at himself in the mirror with satisfaction. He picks up one of the bottles of mineral water standing beside the mirror. He hasn't got an opener and hunts through his pockets in vain. In the end Peter lends him one, and gets it back again. August has now realized he is being laughed at. They each drink a bottle of mineral water and put their hands to their mouths when they burp.

August discovers that his shoelace is undone. He bends down to tie it up. In doing so he knocks his head against Peter's. Peter loses his balance and falls through the frame, after which August realizes that he has been tricked. He is furious and sets off in pursuit of the yelling Peter. Both run out.

The funnel

The white clown calls for a man to help him with an act. At that moment Peter the clown comes past, and the white clown asks whether he would like to earn some money without having to work for it. Peter says he would and asks what he has to do.

White clown: 'Well, here is a funnel.'

Peter: 'What are we supposed to do with it?'

White clown: 'Put it inside your trousers.'

Peter: 'What do you mean? Put it inside my trousers?'

Clowns as weight-lifters. See section on weight-lifting, p. 91.

White clown: 'Yes.' (He puts the funnel, an ordinary kitchen funnel, in position so that the mouth of the funnel stretches out the trouser band.)

Peter: 'Ooh, it tickles!'

White clown: 'Never mind that. Now look, you stand there, and here is a coin, which I am going to put on your forehead. When I count 1–2–3, you nod your head, and if the coin falls into the funnel, it's yours, but if it falls on the ground, it's mine.'

Peter stands a little behind the white clown with the coin on his forehead and the funnel in his trouser band, and the white clown starts counting. But as Peter stands there gazing up into the air, the white clown picks up a little watering can and, while he counts, pours down into the funnel.

White clown: '1–2 . . . '

Peter: 'Help! I'm getting wet. I'm getting wet.' (He is afraid the coin will fall down by the side of the funnel. He is angry with the white clown and wants to clobber him, but the white clown won't let him.)

White clown: 'Now, now, now! It's only a joke. But look

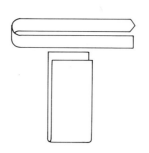 

This is how the bag for the clown's bottle is made. A strip of leather is used for the belt. It is fastened with a button, so that it fits tightly, for the bottle is heavy when it is full of water.

there. There's August coming. You do the act with him and you'll see.'

Peter calls August over and now he plays the part of the white clown. He asks whether August wants to earn some money without having to work for it. August says he does. But Peter is too eager and keeps talking about getting water down the funnel, while the white clown tries to shut him up. In the end the white clown takes over the job, and now he is just about to stick the funnel down August's trousers.

White clown: 'Well, August, now you are going to earn some money without having to work for it. Just you see. But first we must push this funnel down your trousers.'

August: 'What! Have I really got to have that funnel in my trousers? Oh I feel so embarrassed. Can't I turn my back while I push it in?'

White clown: 'Well, never mind that, but hurry up. There, now stand still. Look, here is a coin that I am going to lay on your forehead. And now put your head back, and when I count 1–2–3, you nod your head. If the coin falls down into the funnel, it is yours, but if it falls on the floor it's mine. Are you ready?'

August: 'Yes, get going.'

The white clown now starts counting slowly up to three, at the same time pouring water into the funnel. Peter cannot understand why no water comes out through the trouser leg. He crawls round on the floor and peers up through the trouser leg, but there is not a drop of water. The white clown is also very astonished, and when at last he says 'three', August nods his head and the coin falls down into the funnel. August collects the money and puts it in his pocket.

White clown: 'But August, didn't you notice anything?'

August: 'Yes, I noticed that I had earned a coin.'

Peter: 'Yes, but what about the water?'

August: 'Oh, the water. Yes, I've got it here.' (He hauls a bottle almost full of water out of his trousers. The bottle hangs in a bag that had previously been fixed to a belt inside his trousers.)

The clown's sweethearts

August goes round the edge of the ring waving affectionately to the ladies in the audience and counting.

White clown: 'Look here, you! What are you up to? You can't go round pointing your finger at the audience like that!'

August: 'I'm not. I'm counting my sweethearts.'

White clown: 'Counting your sweethearts? What nonsense are you going to talk next. You aren't going to try and tell me that you, with your red nose, have any sweethearts here!'

August: 'Oh yes, I have! Can't you see all those pretty young ladies sitting there. They are my sweethearts, all of them, and I can prove it.'

White clown: 'Your sweethearts! How can you prove it?'

August: 'Well, I'll show you. I'm going to ask all the ladies who are *not* my sweethearts to say so.'

White clown: 'How are you going to do that? Try – just you try.'

August: 'All right. I shall ask all the ladies who are not my sweethearts to lift their left legs up to their right ears! There, you can see for yourself! There is not a single one who says she isn't, so they are all my sweethearts!'

The glass of gin

A small table has been brought into the ring, perhaps made from a packing case. The white clown and August stand talking together.

White clown: 'I feel like a glass of gin.'

August: 'Yes, that's a good idea.'

White clown: 'Yes, but have you got the money for a glass of gin?'

August: 'No, I haven't.'

At this moment a circus hand comes in with a bottle of gin in one hand and a saucer with a glass on it in the other.

White clown: 'How much is it?'

Circus hand: 'It costs ten pence.'

White clown: 'Right, then I will have a glass.'

The circus hand pours out a glass and places it and the saucer on the table, and the white clown pays.

August: 'Hey, can't I have a glass too?'

1

2

3

August is offered the glass of gin after it has been turned over, as shown in figs. 1–3. The way the white clown turns it right way up again is shown in figs. 4, 5 and 6, and so far, so good. But he is silly enough to let go of the glass when it is back in position as in fig. 1, and then August pinches the glass – with one hand.

Circus hand: 'Yes, if you've got ten pence.'

August: 'What did you say? Ten pence for a thimbleful like that? No, I haven't got that much money.'

White clown: 'All right, then you can't have a glass of gin. If you haven't got any money, you can't have any gin.'

August: 'Can't I just! Can't I have any gin without money! Well, I'd have you know I can drink that glass of gin that's just under your nose there, without you seeing it.'

White clown: 'What did you say? Oh no, you can't.'

August: 'Oh yes, I can. Shall we bet on it?'

White clown: 'Yes, we might as well, if you insist on losing your money.'

August: 'All right, how much shall we bet? A hundred pounds?'

White clown: 'A hundred pounds, no, no, no, August. Not a hundred pounds, that's much too much.'

August: 'Not quite so much then? What about five pence?'

They bet, August seizes the glass and drinks the gin.

White clown: 'Yes, but August, I saw you!'

August: 'What, you saw me? Then hang me if I don't have to give you five pence. That was a nice cheap gin anyway! Five pence! And it ought to cost ten pence!'

White clown: 'Yes, but August, you tricked me.'

August: 'Yes, I did, didn't I.'

White clown: 'You tricked me, and I'm angry with you. But it doesn't matter, for now I'm going to give you a glass all the same, but on condition that you use only one hand to drink it. Now we shall see.'

The white clown calls the circus hand, who comes and fills the glass and is given ten pence by the white clown.

August: 'Ah!'

White clown: 'There you are, August. This glass of gin is for you, but remember, you must use only one hand!'

August (facing the audience): 'Well, that's easy enough, I never use more than one hand when I drink gin. Ee, this ought to be good, I love gin.' (Rubs his stomach.)

Meanwhile the white clown has picked up the saucer, turned it over and laid it upside down over the glass. With a quick twist he turns both of them over, so that the glass stands bottom upwards on the saucer.

White clown: 'You can turn it downside up!'

August (turning to the white clown): 'Thanks very much! That's just the job. Cheers, everyone! I say, what's the matter?

The floating clown. The clown walks along the ground with his head thrown well back. In front of him he carries a light wooden form in the shape of a ladder. There are pieces of material wound round the legs of the ladder, so that they look like the clown's. The shoes are tied to the ends. A cushion is laid on top of the form, to look like the clown's stomach when a rug has been laid over it.

4

5

What on earth is the matter? It's upside down!'

White clown: 'You can turn it downside up!'

August: 'And with only one hand?'

White clown: 'Yes!'

August tries several times and with all sorts of gestures to find out what to do, but without success. He even looks under the table, to see if he can find any help there.

August: 'No, it beats me. I give up.'

White clown: 'Well, just you watch, August. I hold the saucer with the glass of gin on it *with one hand*. Then I bend forward a little and put my forehead against the glass and straighten up quickly and throw my head back, so that the glass is balanced on my forehead. Then I put the saucer down on the table *with one hand* and take the glass *with one hand* and set it on the saucer *with one hand*.'

August: 'And then I drink the gin *with one hand*!' (He grabs the glass and drinks up quickly, then runs out of the ring, pursued by the white clown.)

6

The bet

White clown: 'Ladies and gentlemen. I am an expert at betting, and I want to get in touch with someone who would dare to bet with me.'

At this moment the clown Peter comes into the ring. The white clown goes over to him and asks for his help.

White clown: 'Now listen to me. I want to bet you that you can't bend over and pick up a coin from that plate on the ground there, without saying anything.'

Peter: 'Yes, of course I can.'

They each lay a coin on the plate, and Peter bends down to pick the money up, but the white clown immediately kicks him in the backside.

Peter: 'Ow! ow!'

White clown: 'There you are, Peter. You said 'ow'. You've lost. The money's mine.' (The white clown takes the money and puts it in his pocket.)

At this moment August comes ambling into the ring. The white clown catches sight of him.

White clown: 'Hey, August! Do you want to bet with me?'

And August says he will. They discuss the conditions at length and eventually agree. Then August bends down to pick the money up. Peter and the white clown get ready to give him a good kick, but just at that moment August raises his long jacket to reveal that he has a board with long nails in it fixed to the back of his trousers. So the two clowns dare not kick him, and August picks up the money and puts it in his pocket, grinning. The two other clowns are furious that they have lost the bet.

Trick cyclists

It is usually boys who are keenest on doing tricks on bicycles. Many of them can 'cycle backwards', standing on the pedals and leaning back against the handlebars, pedalling the wrong way round. You steer by twisting your body from side to side.

You can also have two riding at once, each on one pedal. The one on the right of the bike has his left foot on the pedal,

and vice versa. It looks funny when they ride, because the two of them bob up and down like a couple of pistons. The trick is not to ride too quickly, as then the cycle gets out of control.

The mini-cycle

The saddle of a mini-cycle can be screwed almost completely down, and then the artist can ride with someone smaller on his shoulders. Or someone who is good at keeping his balance can sit on the handlebars with his legs in front, while his partner pedals and steers. Someone else can also stand on the carrier at the back and hold on to the cyclist's shoulders as he rides, or with a little practice he can stand there without holding on. The last two turns can be combined, so that there are three performers working on the same cycle.

The mono-cycle

It looks difficult to ride a cycle with only one wheel, but in fact is is not so very hard.

Any smith can make a mono-cycle. The only necessity is that the wheel must be small, so that the movable part of the apparatus, the axle, comes as low as possible. An ordinary-sized wheel is too big. The best thing would be the front wheel of a goods cycle or a wheel from a mini-cycle.

The trick in mounting a mono-cycle and getting started is

A mono-cycle. A pair of ordinary shorts can easily be converted into a striking item of the artiste's dress.

83

to hold on tightly to the front of the saddle with one hand and keep the other hand stretched out at your side as a balancing weight. At the same time move the pedals into the right position under you, and the moment you have the cycle steady, slip your hand away from the saddle and hold that out as well as a balancing weight. Now bend forward slightly and pedal vigorously, so that the cycle moves forward.

At the beginning it is important to have your weight forwards, so that you don't lose your balance and strike your back against the ground. Take care to fall forwards when you fall. And you will fall. Many times.

Each time the saddle will hit against the ground, before you have time to grab it. This can be avoided if you wear a loose rubber belt, perhaps a strip of cycle tyre, tied round your waist. As you get up on the cycle, draw the rubber band round the saddle, so that it will stay on when you fall. A strip of leather or fabric round the waist is no good, as it would not stretch when you come off, and you could hurt yourself.

Once you have learnt to ride a mono-cycle you can perform all sorts of elegant turns on it.

Other cycling acts

'Equestrian acts' can also be done on cycles. With a little practice the performer can learn to pick up a flower or a scarf from the ground as he rides round the ring. Remember, as in an equestrian act, to ride the right way round.

The same trick cyclist could also ride through a large wooden frame over which lining paper, newspaper or something of the sort has been stretched and stuck down. The paper must not be too strong. It could be decorated with figures or painted to look like a large shooting target. The frame is held by two circus hands. (Lining paper can be bought in quite wide rolls, which saves you the trouble of sticking several pieces together.)

Tightrope walking

Tightrope walking is difficult, whether the rope is tight or slack. It is easiest on a tight rope.

But as there is no time to spend several months training, you must think up something else, for there must be some kind of tightrope walking in your circus.

Take a long, firm plank of wood and nail a thick rope along one of the narrow sides. Then lay the plank on top of a couple of tall packing cases with the rope facing the audience, and and the tightrope is ready.

It doesn't matter if the audience can see what you have done, for as soon as the tightrope walker has started his performance, the audience will forget that they have been tricked a little.

There are several kinds of tightrope walking. Here are a few possibilities. There is the elegant, butterfly-like dancer with a parasol, who dances gracefully backwards and forwards.

Then there is the vagabond, who has terrible difficulty in getting up on to the supports. He manages in the end by dint of lifting his stiff legs up with his hands. Once on the rope he does all sorts of neck-breaking things and falls off several times. In the end he is driven out by the ring-master, who cannot endure his miserable performance any longer.

Or you could do a different sort of parody of tightrope walking.

Immediately after a graceful act in which a dancer has almost hovered along the rope, a clown comes wandering into the ring with a torn old umbrella in one hand and a coil of rope in the other. He throws the umbrella down on the ground and lays the rope out across the ring. Then he snatches up his umbrella in passing, works his way along the rope and makes fun of the graceful dancer by clumsily imitating his or her movements.

But a crazy clown can also go about things more seriously. He can show how difficult tightrope walking is. He can hardly scrape up the courage to start out, and he squats down repeatedly. But he tries again, as he is determined to master it. He stands out on the rope and nearly loses his balance and is very relieved when he actually gets safely across.

But take care not to drag this sort of act out too long, or it may easily turn out to be boring.

Who says that a rope has to be up in the air at all costs at a children's circus! You can lay a balancing plank on the ground as shown in the drawing. Then you can lay on a wonderful tightrope act, and it doesn't matter if the tightrope walker

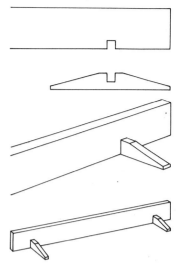

A good balancing bar can be made with a couple of supports.

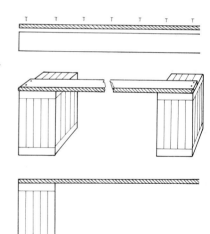

At the top, the rope – a thick rope – nailed to the edge of a plank. In the middle, the plank set between two packing cases. At the bottom, the set-up as seen by the audience, if they have the rope more or less at eye level.

occasionally steps off it a bit or loses his balance, because the audience can't see.

It is best to wear light gym shoes for tightrope walking or shoes with rubber soles.

Trapeze and rings

It is possible to show trapeze and ring acts only if the apparatus can be set up in the ring with 100 per cent safety. The best way would be to build the circus up in front of a fixed swing or clothes-drying stand, if this is possible. (See picture on front cover.)

If you have to use an improvised stand, do get a grown-up to inspect it from the point of view of safety, so that no one falls and hurts himself because the stand falls over or collapses.

A number of acts can be done with both trapeze and rings. You can do swallows' nests and upward swings. You can

Two trapeze artistes in the air. It is very important for a trapeze to be completely safe. The ropes with the knots at the side of the posts are climbing ropes. The two pictures are from the Circus Zoo, Nykøbing Falster.

hang by both legs and by one leg and possibly by the toes. If one acrobat is hanging by his legs, another can hang from his arms and do somersaults.

Here is an idea for a Chinese act which does not require a stand for the trapeze. Two strong Chinamen walk into the ring carrying a pole over their shoulders. They stand on either side of the ring, and an acrobat comes forward, bows and performs trapeze acts on the pole.

Magic

Magic comes off best, as a rule, if presented on a permanent stage where the audience has a chance of seeing the act from the front.

Long-winded thought-transference turns and complicated card-tricks usually bore a circus audience, so it is better not to experiment with that sort of thing. The circus calls for speed, so a magician has to be very good to live up to that standard.

Arrange short acts, which you can read up in books on magic bought at a bookshop or borrowed from a library.

You can either make the accessories yourselves or buy them in special shops.

The oldest and most important requirement for a magician is a magic wand, which is a round stick $\frac{3}{8}$ in. $-\frac{1}{2}$ in. thick and 10–12 in. long. It is painted black, and when it is dry the ends are painted white about 2 in. down.

The magic wand is used among other things to distract the attention of the audience from what the magician is doing, but the wand itself can disappear.

The disappearing magician's wand

An exact copy of the magician's wand is made out of a piece of black paper and a piece of white, shiny paper. The black paper must be about 4 in. wide and the same length as the wand. It is rolled round the wand and glued together. A piece of white paper 2 in. wide is rolled round the ends of the black case and stuck on. The case is now pulled off the wand, and the ends are blocked with two wooden stoppers $\frac{3}{4}$ in. long, which are glued in.

Before coming into the ring the magician hides the real wand somewhere on his person. He might, for example, push it down inside one stocking.

The magician likes to work with a little table on which he has his accessories. Our magician has a magician's table in the ring, and on this he places, among other things, the fake wand.

He bows to the audience and says that it is a great pleasure for him to have the opportunity of entertaining them for a few minutes with one or two conjuring tricks, and to begin with he would like to show them how to make a magic wand disappear.

He now picks up the magic wand and, as it were accidentally, strikes the end of it against the table or something hard, so that the audience is convinced that it is a real magic wand.

Then he takes a big piece of newspaper, pushes up his sleeves and carefully rolls up the paper wand in the newspaper. Then he shows the audience the package and says that he is going to make it disappear. He crumples up the parcel and throws it to the back of the ring, where a circus hand removes it.

He now makes a few mysterious arm movements, uttering a few magic formulae: 'Hokus pokus filiokus filihankat! Simsalabim bambasaladusaladim!'

And he goes on to say: 'Yes, ladies and gentlemen. You have seen how I made my magic wand disappear, but now I am going to have the pleasure of producing it again, for a magician cannot, of course, manage without his wand.'

He holds his left arm tightly pressed against his body and says: 'Yes, I can see quite clearly from the look of you all that you think I have the wand in here (*he raises his left arm, but keeps his right arm pressed against his body*), and the gentleman down there in the third row has just whispered to his neighbour that I've got the wand under my right arm (*raises the arm*), but that is not the case. No, ladies and gentlemen, if you have been following what I have been doing correctly, you will have observed that it is here.'

The magician produces the wand from his stocking and holds it up to the audience, bowing.

The vanishing egg

The egg bag that has a secret pocket is another very old magician's accessory. It is made of soft black material according to the pattern shown in the drawing.

A china egg will also be required. This can be bought quite cheaply from a pet shop or ironmonger's.

The act begins with the magician picking up the bag, which is lying on the table, and showing it to the audience. He tells them that the bag is empty and proves it by turning it quickly inside out and back again.

Then he takes the china egg and puts it inside the bag with the audience watching. He utters a few magic formulae, and a moment later demonstrates that the bag is empty by turning it inside out again. (The egg is hidden in the secret pocket, which the magician holds in his hand as he holds the bag.)

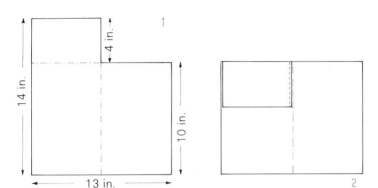

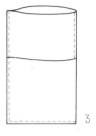

He carefully relaxes his grip on the egg, which slips down into the bag. Whatever was that? The magician peers into the bag, takes the egg out and shows it to the audience. Then he makes it disappear again into the bag, which again is shown empty to the audience.

A circus hand now places a high stool in the ring, and the magician asks a member of the audience to stand on this with his back turned to the audience.

He asks his assistant to bend forward and say: 'Cockadoodle-doo, I can lay an egg! Cockadoodledoo, I can lay an egg!'

At the same time the magician holds the bag under his assistant's back. Lo and behold! There really is an egg in the bag.

The assistant is asked to take it out and show it to the audience himself.

Now it has to vanish again, and the assistant puts it back in the bag. The magician announces that the egg has disappeared, and shows that it has in the usual way, but holding one arm very obviously close against his body, so that the audience think he has the egg hidden there. They ask to see what he is hiding, but there is nothing there. Now the other arm looks as though it is hiding the egg, but there is nothing there either!

Then he asks his assistant to blow (no, not to spit!) into the bag and lets him feel whether the egg is there. Yes, there it is in the bag, and the assistant shows it to the audience, while the magician bows.

He takes the egg and lays it back on the table together with the bag, while the assistant returns to his place.

The magic bottle

For this little act you need two beer bottles, two pieces of rope and a small piece of indiarubber or cork, cut down to the size of a very large pea.

The magician asks a member of the audience to come into the ring. He hands him one of the pieces of rope and a bottle and tells him to do exactly the same as the magician, for the purpose of the act is to make the bottles swing.

The assistant is not, of course, provided with the indiarubber ball, which is the whole secret.

The magician drops the ball unnoticed into his bottle and tells the assistant to do exactly the same as him.

The magician carefully pushes his rope about halfway down into the bottle. The assistant does the same. Each of them takes his bottle and turns it upside down, pulling a little at the cord.

Then they both reverse their bottles, and the magician says a magic formula which the assistant repeats, and the bottles should now be able to swing. The magician's does, but the assistant merely pulls his piece of rope out of the bottle.

The magician's bottle is so firmly fixed that he can even swing it carefully backwards and forwards by the rope.

'Well, well,' says the magician, 'you must have got a bad bottle, so let's change over.'

He pushes the rope down into the bottle to loosen the little piece of indiarubber or cork that has held it firmly against the neck of the bottle. He slips the ball discreetly into his hand as he pulls out the rope and drops it into the other bottle. The act is repeated with the same result.

The balloon that changes colour

Buy two balloons of different colours. You now have to put one balloon inside the other. You can do this by sticking the pointed end of a long pencil down into the balloon that is

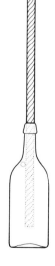

The little ball prevents the rope slipping out.

lightest in colour and that has to go inside. Carefully work it into place inside the other one. Now blow up both balloons at the same time and tie them up. Do not blow the balloons up too far, as there is a danger then that people might see the one inside through the other one.

First show the balloon to the audience. The change of colour happens when the magician carefully pricks a hole with a pin in the outside balloon, which bursts with a bang. But take care not to prick too deep! It might be a good idea to have a double balloon in reserve.

The magician can now end his part of the performance by standing in the centre of the ring and saying: 'And now, ladies and gentlemen, I am going to show you a very great vanishing act (*pause*). I am going to vanish out of the ring (myself)' (*bows out*).

Weight-lifting

For this you need a number of accessories that you can make yourselves.

You will need loose weights. These are made of 'gauze mâché' or papier mâché over large jam jars or pails, which are removed from the dry mâché before the casts are closed at the ends. They are painted black, and various figures are painted in white on the weights according to size: 200 lb., 300 lb., 400 lb.

Weights with a bar between are made in the same way, or they can be sawn out of a plank of wood and mounted at the end of a round pole about 3 ft. long. These too are painted black with or without figures.

If the act is to have the planned effect, you will need two or three sets with various sizes of weight on.

These accessories can be replaced by a single bar with interchangeable weights. The two largest weights are fixed permanently to the bar about 10 in. from the ends. The loose weights with holes through them can then be placed on the bar until the weight-lifter cannot manage any more.

The weight-lifting act is best presented by an athlete in a white vest with long sleeves padded out with swelling cottonwool muscles. He can wear a very wide belt round his waist (made of fabric), a big, black, handle-bar moustache and medals on his chest (paper medals can be bought in joke shops, or you can make them yourselves). He should look like an athlete from the 1890s.

The handle of the weights is a piece of unravelled rope which is stuck on with papier mâché. The weights are painted black or with metallic paint when they are finished, and the numbers of kilos or pounds are painted on.

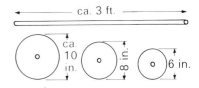

Approximate sizes for hand-weights.

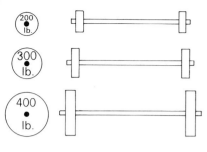

Three hand-weights with discs fixed on.

Hand-weight with three inter-changeable discs. To prevent the discs falling off, they can be fixed with nails inside and out.

The weight bars and the loose weights are carried into the ring in advance by the whole staff of circus hands, who have great difficulty with the heavy objects. It takes two of them to drag the heaviest ones.

Now the world-famous strong man and weight-lifter comes out. He bows to the audience with dignity, walks up and down once or twice and is hardly able to move because of his huge muscles. He bends his arms and proudly shows the bulging muscles.

He lifts the weights with great difficulty. He can more or less manage the smaller ones, but the big ones are hard to get up. But he does succeed. At the end he bows again to the audience with a majestic air and leaves the ring, waving an upraised arm in farewell.

Then a circus hand comes rushing in from behind the curtain. He can well be the smallest and frailest-looking one. He clearly hasn't understood a thing and just snatches up all the weights and bars and runs carelessly out with them in his arms.

The weight-lifter and strong man can dress up his act with a little by-play.

For this he needs a stick of liquorice and a piece of iron of the same thickness and length painted black. These are both laid in a prettily painted box.

The strong man shows the piece of iron to the audience and tells them that among his minor talents is the ability to bend it. He hands it over to the audience, and one or two of the strongest men try to bend it but fail.

The strong man now takes it back and lays it back in the box, explaining that he must pick up a few weights first to loosen his muscles.

A little while later he opens the box and this time takes out the liquorice which, with a great display of effort, he bends into a ring. He shows it to the audience, puts it straight back in the box and closes the lid.

If it is not possible to get hold of a suitable piece of liquorice, a piece of lead or plastic cable painted black will do instead. This can be got from an electrician's.

Large Children's Circuses

There are two permanent children's circuses in Scandinavia: one at Furuvik in Sweden and one at Odense in Denmark.

There is another in the children's republic of Bemposta in Spain, but these seem to be the only ones in the whole of Europe.

So a big children's circus is a rarity.

Sweden

Furuvik's Park south of Gävle started in 1900 as a modest pleasure ground with swings, roundabouts and a beautiful bathing beach. It went on like this for a number of years, but in 1936 part of the park was turned into a zoo, and after that it changed little by little until it is now a well-frequented amusement park with a zoo and a number of attractions.

One of these is the children's circus. It began with a troupe of children who used to do folk-dancing every year from 1936 onwards. Every now and then the leader of the 'Furuvik children', the head gardener Johan Jansson, would pick a boy or girl out of the troupe.

They would sing a little song, perform a solo act or whatever it might be, and so the idea of performing little plays and presenting circus acts arose.

In 1940 the children were provided with a new theatre-cum-circus with an indoor ring of $12\frac{1}{2}$ yd. and arranged in the usual circus style with wooden benches all round. The children now usually appear on a big open-air stage with wings behind and benches in front. There is room for 1,500 spectators. The indoor 'circus' stage is used only in bad weather.

Johan Jansson led the children for the first twenty-five years up to 1965, when his place was taken by the park inspector, Bodo West-Rosenberg.

The troupe, which travels a fair amount in Sweden, consists of about fifty children between the ages of seven and fifteen. The performance lasts an hour and includes acrobatics, singing and dancing.

Denmark

Odense Zoological Gardens were opened on 10 May 1930.

In 1947 the director, Christian Jensen, and the inspector of the gardens, Herold Nielsen, went on a study tour of Sweden. They visited, among other places, the zoological gardens at Furuvik, and here they saw a permanent children's circus for the first time. They thought it was a good idea, and when they came home they immediately set about organizing a similar children's circus.

The Circus Zoo gave its first performance on 17 May 1948 and celebrated its silver jubilee season in 1972.

To begin with the circus was in the Zoo-Tivoli premises, where there were already swings, roundabouts and other such installations. The ring was 11 yds. across, and the children changed in a temporary building under primitive conditions. Space was cramped, but two years later the circus moved into the Zoological Gardens. Here conditions are ideal with a building designed for the purpose.

And there it still is. The open-air ring is 13 yds. across, and the seats are arranged in steps round the ring. There is room for about 600 people.

Inspector Herold Neilsen became the leader, and has been so ever since.

Every spring the Circus Zoo advertises in the newspapers for children as performers and other personnel. From the large numbers that apply forty to fifty are chosen, and after a couple of months' thorough training they run the performances themselves, with Herold Nielsen standing discreetly in the background.

The main thing in the eyes of the authorities is that the performers and personnel should enjoy themselves and, so to speak, play their way through the performances, rather than that the acts should be performed perfectly. The audience takes the same attitude and reacts unfavourably if one of the same attitude and reacts unfavourably if one of the performers is too big or if a grown-up takes part.

The Circus Zoo has gone on a number of tours inside Denmark, but prefers to remain on its home ground. Performances take place every Sunday afternoon all through the summer and during the school holidays on Tuesdays too, and last about an hour.

Spain

The Spanish children's circus has its home in the village of Bemposta in the province of Galicia.

Here in 1956 a Catholic priest, Jesus Silva, founded a whole children's village, which he called the Republic of Bemposta, with about 1,000 orphan children as inhabitants. There are only twenty-four adults in the republic and they have no voice in the council.

Pastor Silva's parents were circus people. He himself was born in a circus and appeared as a performer when he was a boy.

In 1965 he started a school for circus artistes in the children's village.

Older circus performers thought that the idea was a brilliant one, so they got together to teach their art to the children.

After five years' preparation and hard training the circus was ready to give a performance before an audience. And now about eighty-five children and young people from eleven to eighteen drive round in battered old lorries which they have decorated themselves.

They are a tremendous success all over Spain and earn lots of money for the children's village. In 1971 the circus appeared for the first time outside Spain.